D1557393

TO THE RIVER

DON GILLMOR

TO THE RIVER

LOSING MY BROTHER

RANDOM HOUSE CANADA

PUBLISHED BY RANDOM HOUSE CANADA

Copyright © 2018 Don Gillmor

www.penguinrandomhouse.ca

Library and Archives Canada Cataloguing in Publication

Gillmor, Don, author
   To the river : losing my brother / Don Gillmor.

Issued in print and electronic formats.
ISBN 978-0-345-81466-1
eBook ISBN 978-0-345-81468-5

   1. Gillmor, David. 2. Gillmor, David—Death and burial. 3. Suicide
victims—Canada—Biography. 4. Suicide—Psychological aspects. I. Title.

HV6548.C3G55 2018   362.28092   C2018-904534-5
                                              C2018-904535-3

Book design by Five Seventeen
Cover image: © saemilee / Getty Images
Photo on page v courtesy of the author

Printed and bound in the United States of America

10 9 8 7 6 5 4 3 2 1

Penguin
Random House
RANDOM HOUSE CANADA

For David

The calm,
Cool face of the river
Asked me for a kiss.

"Suicide's Note"
Langston Hughes

We are, above all, eternal spectators looking upon,
    never from,
the place itself. We are the
essence of it. We construct it.
It falls apart. We reconstruct it
and fall apart ourselves.

"The Eighth Duino Elegy"
Rainer Maria Rilke

The air is cold, but the sleeping pills have made you heavy and dull and you don't feel it. You're out of cigarettes. It snowed last night, a light dusting. There is ice on the river but the centre is open, the current sluggish. You take off your hat and gently place it on the ground. The sun is already behind the hills in early afternoon, darkness closing in the way it does this far north in December. The distance to the open water is shorter than you think, and you stare at the river for five minutes (was it fifteen?), the surface dark and changeable. There are no thoughts left, only a faint melody. You take one more step and the river carries you away.

1

THE RIVER

When we were children, my mother warned my brother, David, and I about the Red River, which flowed muddily near our house in Winnipeg, just beyond a wooded area thick with mystery. *Don't go near the river.*

Inevitably, I gravitated to it. I sat with friends in the limbs of trees near the edge of the water, playing with Zippo lighters, analyzing superheroes. Poor Batman protected only by his wealth and his toys. A superhero without superpowers.

"Spiderman could swat him like a fly."

"Superman could swat Spiderman like a fly."

"Spiderman holding *kryptonite?*"

"Thor could take them both."

"Thor's not even a real guy."

My brother was two and a half years younger than me, and our mother would regularly utter the words most older brothers dread: *Take your little brother with you.* So he would sit with us, a boy without guile, without information about the world (originally there had been eight Beatles but four died mysteriously, a friend told us with authority). A burden.

In spring, the mud-coloured Red gained momentum as the snow melted. Every spring we watched it rise, hopeful and fearful at the same time, wanting some drama in our lives but afraid of the consequences. Before we were born, in the Great Flood of 1950, the Red River rose more than thirty feet and produced an ad hoc lake that was sixty miles long. It swallowed our house, though it belonged to someone else then. Our whole neighbourhood was evacuated, among the hundred thousand Winnipeggers who had to leave their homes. Bob Hope gave an impassioned plea for aid on his show, which debuted that year. Princess Elizabeth, the future Queen of England, and her husband, the Duke of Edinburgh, came to our neighbourhood to view the damage, the start of their lengthy careers viewing colonial wreckage and parades. Every spring the Great Flood was invoked; the waters could rise and swallow us all.

Our neighbourhood, Wildwood Park, was contained in a loop in the river and bordered by a forest, a golf course and a private boys' school. In the summer, parents simply opened the doors in the morning and we disappeared for the rest of the day. Sports rose and fell, baseball games, ball hockey games. Cliques formed and splintered. In the evening we played kick the can until after dark when our mothers finally called us home.

A staple was guns. "Do you want to play guns?" someone would say. And kids would race home and return with their latest plastic weapons. Except my brother and me. Our mother wouldn't let us own toy guns, a revolutionary and unwelcome stance in the 1960s. We were the least dangerous kids for miles.

"Everyone else has one," I told my mother.

"You're not everyone else," she said.

"What am I supposed to use to defend myself?"

"You can use a stick."

A stick. Armed with a stick, and sent out against machine guns and grenade launchers. It didn't matter that none of those guns—the cap guns, the lever action Winchester rifles, the plastic grenades that were supposed to explode on impact—behaved the way they did in commercials. A stick was, in fact, a more effective weapon. But the game of guns, insofar as it was an actual game, was about recreating the heroics of war. Crawling around the dogwood bushes with a toy rifle and a plastic knife in your belt lent an authenticity to the experience that a stick failed to do.

Not being able to buy guns removed a fundamental part of the game for my brother and me—the tactile joy of that plastic hardware. There was more fun to be found in the acquiring of weapons than in actually using them. In 1964, when the first Johnny Seven OMA (One Man Army) arrived in my neighbourhood with its seven functions (anti-tank rocket, anti-bunker missile, repeating rifle, grenade launcher, Tommy gun, automatic pistol, armour-piercing shell), it started an arms race. Every parent heard roughly the same arguments that the Pentagon was giving to Congress in the wake of the Cuban Missile Crisis: in order to survive in a dangerous world we need more weaponry, which means more money, which means a world safe for democracy.

Neither my brother nor I was comforted by the fact that the plastic bullets from the Johnny Seven started their downward trajectory pretty much right out of the barrel and the grenades only launched a few feet in what seemed like slow motion. As pedants pointed out in the critical death tally that ran through our gun narrative ("I got you!" "Did not! I got *you*!"), if it had been a real grenade, the launcher would have been blown up along with the target.

"But it wasn't a real grenade."

"If it wasn't real, then how can I be dead?"

This line of inquiry often ended in an almost Foucauldian deconstruction of the fantasy we inhabited, which was, after all, held up only by unanimous belief. A single doubter could throw our whole world into question. We were dead or alive by consensus. Some, like my little brother, refused to die, regardless of how blatant the hit, how proximate the grenade, how many reliable witnesses confirmed it. He wouldn't acknowledge the red streak on his chest where the plastic knife had torn out his heart. He refused death, arguing that while he had suffered a *wound,* certainly, it hadn't been fatal because his years of guerilla training had made him all but immune to flesh wounds. Or he had managed to put up an invisible force field developed by the military only hours earlier that had deflected the plastic bullets. We all wanted to live. To die was to be excluded for the rest of the game. And though the game was ill defined and interspersed with stretches of boredom and confusion and frustration and malfunctioning equipment, we wanted to be a part of it.

Maybe it wasn't even a game. There were few rules, no referees, and no reliable way of keeping score. Occasionally our debates over who was dead descended into actual fighting. When this happened we left the battlefield and went home and turned on the black and white television in the living room to find something like Jack LaLanne's exercise show, then turned it off and got out the comics and lay on the floor and reread them.

Then we'd get bored and drift down to the slippery clay banks of the Red River, which had a decayed vegetal smell. Occasionally we pulled small crayfish out of the muck, blind and grey, and examined them. In a small clearing we once found a mouldy blanket and an empty package of cigarettes and two condoms, evidence of a crime we couldn't entirely articulate. Perhaps a famous actress had been there, or someone's mother. We abandoned that mystery and climbed a tree near the water, where we sat on a limb, watching for bodies floating up from crime-riddled America.

My sister, Alison, arrived six years after David, nine years after me, and the family geometry shifted, with David now the middle child. And it meant he and I had to share a bedroom. He was an eccentric roommate. One night I heard him get up and go downstairs. My mother heard him too and found David in the living room, still fast asleep, urinating on our television set. He developed an odd habit of thumping his head against his pillow. He did it to get to sleep, he told me, which seemed counterproductive.

"Stop thumping."

"I can't get to sleep."

"Well, now *I* can't get to sleep."

Thump thump thump.

Our shared bedroom and forced proximity produced ongoing arguments over space, chores, toys and bands (Who would be bigger—the Beatles or the Dave Clark Five? I argued for the DC5) and who owned the magnetic puck hockey set that featured players for the Leafs and Canadiens tethered to long, thin rods. It had been given to both of us by Santa Claus, but I felt it was directed more at me. I was the hockey player, after all, the one who was out there on the ice in minus-twenty weather, who had read Gordie Howe's book *Hockey . . . Here's Howe!* We played the hockey game maniacally, slapping the magnetic puck so hard it jumped off the miniature rink and rolled across the floor. We would play checkers until it became clear that David was going to lose and I was going to gloat, and then he'd clear the board with a sweep of his arm and say it didn't count because we didn't finish.

We took piano lessons together from a patient man who guided us through short, standard passages. My brother went first and I could hear his alarming progress, moving from scales to Chopin in what seemed like a montage while I was in the next room, pondering the unfairness of my brother's musical gift. At the piano I approached each note separately, relieved to be past it, fearful of the next one. I was almost three years older and this imbalance irked. Our lovely Steinway piano became a refuge for David when other endeavours failed him (sports, for example). After a few years, the piano teacher told my parents they needed to find a better teacher for my brother because he had a gift. "You're wasting your money with the other one," he said.

I'm chasing my brother across the length of our vast unmown lawn, closing on him. We've been in this house for a few months, a rambling sixty-year-old place on a preposterously large lot. It's only a hundred yards from our old house, still inside the idyll of Wildwood. David is heading for the line of trees just before the road. Suddenly he is flipped onto his back, lying in the leaves, his face bloody and terrified. He has run into a rusty wire strung between two trees that has probably been there for decades. The deep cut runs just below his eye and it's off to the emergency ward, not for the first time. For weeks, my mother kept saying, "It's a miracle he wasn't blinded!"

You could say David was accident-prone, though I was

involved in so many of those accidents. Wrestling in our bedroom, his head hitting the iron radiator. There were the wasp stings that David suffered when I knocked down a nest with a hockey stick. He was bitten in the face by a neighbour's dog that had never attacked anyone else. On vacation in Vancouver, he walked into a parking meter.

We once had a pillow fight and our babysitter, a teenager who lived a few doors down, counselled David to swing his pillow from side to side while I swung mine up and down. This Punch and Judy show went on while we bounced on the bed. Then an uppercut with the pillow caught David on the chin and he flew off the bed and cracked his head on the floor, sustaining a concussion.

There was a croquet game that devolved into a blood sport, as so many games between us did. It started with whacking each other's croquet balls out of the yard so that they rolled down the road, and ended with us throwing balls at one another. He hid behind a large tree, then came out and taunted me in that *nyah-nyah* little boy dance. I would throw a croquet ball at him, but by the time the heavy wooden ball had covered the thirty feet, he would be safely behind the tree again. This went on for a while. Finally I yelled an insult *as* I threw the ball, and he fell into my trap, emerging to get nailed in the knee and going down like a sack of potatoes. The possible consequences, which had been so distant and muddy when we began this game, were now suddenly vivid, my little brother writhing on the ground, holding his knee. Bystanders gathered. "Whoa, you killed him!" Then my mother arrived to go through worst-case scenarios with me. "What if it had been his head? Did you think of that? That's the problem, you *didn't* think."

As compensation I designed a game where David tried to throw a basketball into the steel mesh carrier on the front of my bicycle as I repeatedly pedalled by. The initial lobs grew in force, aimed at me rather than the carrier. I pedalled faster and my taunts became more inventive, and David now hurled the basketball at maximum velocity at my head. Inevitably, he connected, knocking me off the bike. I lay on the pavement examining the grit-filled scrapes on my legs, trying to keep tears at bay. My father came out and offered an opinion. "Brilliant game. Really. Why don't you try throwing your hockey sticks into the spokes. That would be even better." That half-beat when we actually entertained this.

My scrapes healed and David recovered from the croquet injury, as he did from so many others. In the winter, I retreated into hockey and he continued to play the piano in our study with infuriating talent, sailing through the Royal Conservatory lessons like Mozart as I fought each note.

I am standing outside our house, tinkering with my stupid bike, a butterfly-handlebarred, banana-seated, sparkly gold, undersized thing with a stick shift on the crossbar. I had paid fifty-six dollars of my own money for it. My parents had argued against it—why not get a full-sized, practical, normal bike? This bike (it had a name, something like Roaring Roadster) was a fad. It would be out of fashion within a year and I would regret it. A month into owner-ship, I realized, painfully, that they were right. The Roaring Roadster was a sad, unreliable novelty with faulty brakes. My only arguments in favour of buying it had been that it was cool in a way my parents could never understand, and that it was my own money and I could buy whatever the hell I wanted. Now I was stuck with an expensive embar-rassment and couldn't afford to buy a normal bike. This lesson in economics and fashion brought on a wave of actual nausea; I was filled with unbearable regret.

My only salvation lay in selling the idea of its coolness to my impressionable little brother, who now had my old bike, a reliable CCM; I decided I'd try and trade my new bike for my old bike.

My parents were away for a few days and my maternal grandmother was taking care of us. Georgina Mainland was a sturdy, pious former Presbyterian who attended the United Church because it was closer, though she held to the no-card-playing-on-Sunday spirit of the Presbyterians. She was warm hearted and bustling and a terrible Scottish cook and believed in cleanliness in all things. She was outside, sweeping the sidewalk, humming something, possibly a hymn.

There was movement above her, on the roof, like a large bird landing. I looked up to see David climbing toward the peak, having taken off the screen in the bathroom window. He straddled the roof and looked directly down at our grandmother. Too close to the edge.

"Georgina Mainland," he said in a deep voice. "This is the voice of God. You have sinned."

My grandmother jumped, some Calvinist fear igniting before she realized that it had to be someone other than God. She looked up and my brother quickly pulled back, though not in time.

"David *Gillmor,* my goodness, *how on earth* . . . Come down from that roof *right now.*"

"Come up and get me."

There was no way Georgie could go up there. For one thing, the bathroom door would be locked from the inside.

"Come down this instant. Or I'll tell your parents."

"They're in Minneapolis."

My grandmother thought about this for a moment. She was far too frugal to actually phone long distance. David was right on the edge, making both of us nervous. If he fell, it would be onto stone and likely onto his head.

"Come down or I'll . . . I'll break your bike!" Georgie shouted.

"You'll *break* my bike?"

Neither of us really knew what this could mean. His bike—my bike, a month earlier—was leaning against the side of the house. She walked over to it and looked up. David leaned dangerously over the edge to look down. She pushed the bike over and it rattled onto the stone.

"Big deal," David said.

My grandmother looked up again, then jumped onto David's bicycle, collapsing the spokes of the rear wheel.

"What are you *doing?* Are you—"

David scrambled away from the edge and I could hear him sliding down the asphalt shingles, heading for the bathroom window. Georgie ran inside to get her wooden spoon.

I walked over to the bicycle, which was, in fact, broken. My plan of five minutes earlier was now thwarted. I could hear the commotion inside, like one of those door-slamming English farces. It ended with David under his covers in our bedroom, Georgie whacking that lump with the wooden spoon.

In summer we often spent a week in Fort Frances, Ontario, a pulp-and-paper town of nine thousand where my father had grown up. It was a four-hour drive east, and we stayed with my grandparents in their large Victorian house. My father's brothers were sometimes there with their families as well. The summer I was thirteen, my brother and I and our cousin Peter went to the Royal Theatre, where we were lightly terrorized by locals, their resentful Milk Duds bouncing off the back of our big-city heads as we watched a starless double bill. One of the movies featured a prison escape, and when we got back to my grandmother's house, my cousin Peter and I knotted sheets together as the prison-ers had. We tied them to the leg of the cot (which looked like a prison cot) in the sunroom on the second floor of the house, then lowered my brother out the window. In the living room below, my grandmother was serving tea to a group of church ladies when David dangled into view through the picture window. The makeshift rope was too short (just like in the movie) and David fell the last six feet, landing in my grandmother's garden.

She rushed out, blaming David for ruining her flowers. My parents bore in on me. "What the *hell* were you thinking? Lowering a ten-year-old out of a second-floor window!"

Once more, the dangers were suddenly obvious. I admitted I hadn't thought it through. A loud lecture followed: Just because it was in a movie didn't mean I should try it with my *ten-year-old brother*, people had been killed climbing out of windows, everyone within a ten-mile radius would think we'd been raised by convicts, it's a *miracle* . . .

A week later we were in the dark foyer of my grandmother's house, getting ready to go fishing for the first time. David took a fishing rod and mock cast it in the hallway, and the fishing hook pierced his ear as it came zipping past. My father had to cut it with wire clippers as David stood there crying. We eventually got out onto the water in a motorboat, uncomfortable in red lifejackets faded to pink, waiting for the walleye, bored. "It's like life," one of the men in the boat explained, "a few moments of excitement followed by lots of nothing."

So it was a happy, if mishap-filled, childhood. It's easy to remember this version of David: guileless, sunny, adventurous, his pale untannable skin, the white-blond hair that was long even in the days of Brylcreem. His musical gift blossomed. He was smart, though not academic. Rebellious in a middle-class way, far from the revolution but still storming some kind of barricade in his head.

When I was sixteen my father was offered a job in Calgary—an opportunity to help create a new faculty at the university—Environmental Design—and he took it. Both David and I were reluctant to move. We'd be going to new schools, would have to make new friends. I was in my last year of high school, David in his last year of middle school. But we embraced the West in our separate ways. I went up to the mountains to ski at every opportunity. David took up the banjo and started playing bluegrass music. He became a student of the genre, bringing home obscure country records, diving into the alternative country world that was burgeoning—Emmylou Harris, the Flying Burrito Brothers, the New Riders of the Purple Sage. He bought cowboy boots, a fancy belt buckle, eventually a cowboy hat and duster, looking like someone out of a spaghetti western. His hair was past his shoulders, a lean young man who was often laughing, always smoking.

We lived on the western edge of the city, with a clear view of the Rocky Mountains. Calgary was the fastest-growing city in North America, the downtown dotted with cranes, subdivisions marching west. The oil boom of the seventies infected all of us with a sense of possibility.

David and I didn't end up in the same school—mine so new it was still under construction—and I didn't see much of him. After high school, I went to university in Calgary, mostly so I could continue to ski. David graduated high school and pursued a musical life, forming a band with some friends. He worked at odd jobs, played music on weekends, smoked a ton of pot. The outgoing child had become a relentlessly social adult, a man who couldn't bear to be alone, and he rarely was. He moved out of our parents' home and moved in with his lovely girlfriend, Carolyn. To my surprise, they got married. It wasn't really a marrying era, and he was young and a counterculture guy. They had a daughter, Ivy, and bought a new car. Suddenly my little brother was a recognizable version of a grown-up. I wasn't at the time, still flailing, dating madly, not sure what I was going to do with my life. And here he was, a husband and father, driving around in a new Honda.

It didn't last. He loved his family but lived for music, playing with friends in someone's house, smoking pot, coming home late. David got divorced, played in a variety of bands and eventually moved to Whitehorse, in the Yukon, 2,300 kilometres north. I moved 2,700 kilometres east to Toronto with the idea of becoming a writer. We hadn't been close when we were in the same city, and now we were separated by half the country. I saw him every few years at most.

My mother acted as a dispatcher, catching everyone up on what everyone else was doing. Her reports on David were always tinged with optimism, though he had long settled into the role of black sheep. He had several different girlfriends who were rated on the maternal scale of how good they would be for him (not very), then a long-term girlfriend who my mother thought was perfect for him. And finally a second wife who aroused my mother's suspicion.

For two decades my relationship with David was defined by distance. I didn't go to Whitehorse, didn't have a physical image of where he lived. I didn't know his friends up there. Though I did imagine his life: playing music in bars, smoking dope, happy in his extended youth.

People often go north to reinvent themselves, to become the person they felt was stifled in Ontario or Indiana. Not everyone embraces its charms. After the first dark winter they return home and put on their old life the way you put on a wet bathing suit on a cold day. I had assumed David would come back from Whitehorse, defeated by the cold if nothing else, but he didn't. He stayed up there for twenty years.

At the age of forty-eight, my brother parked his truck on the side of the Alaska Highway thirty kilometres south of Whitehorse and walked into the Yukon River. On the seat of the truck was an empty bottle of Nytol, the sleep medication. In the cassette deck was a recording of a Calgary band he'd been in. The truck was almost out of gas and the window was open. It was early December and −23°C, the first cold day of the season. The Yukon River was frozen on the sides but still open in the middle. David's cowboy hat was on the ground beside the truck. Footsteps in the snow led to that ribbon of open water.

My brother was a gifted actor with a brilliantly compartmentalized world. He knew half the town, was comfortable in every social strata. People who saw him in those last days said he was in good spirits. I see him standing on that river, a silhouette in the fading afternoon light, and I wonder how he got there.

2

A PERFECT WORLD

In November 2005, three weeks before my brother walked into the river, my father and I were in Pennsylvania to see Frank Lloyd Wright's Fallingwater house. My father is an architect who, as a graduate student in Boston in the 1950s, had heard Wright give a public lecture. He had visited many of Wright's buildings, and he held to many of Wright's principles when he finally designed our family house west of Calgary. But he had never been to Fallingwater, and for his seventy-fifth birthday, I suggested we go together. When I told him this, he got a bit teary; our trip assumed the proportions of a religious pilgrimage.

There had been earlier pilgrimages—including a forced march through the cathedrals of Europe as a teenager on a family trip where my brother and I nodded uncomprehendingly as my father explained flying buttresses and vaulted ceilings. Most of my interest in architecture was the result of living in houses that had been renovated or designed by my father. The idea that design influences behaviour, that it can lead to a better life, has flickered throughout architectural history, liberating the poor from the "rookeries" of nineteenth-century London, giving us elevated public monuments and disastrous public housing developments. Winston Churchill said, "We shape our buildings and afterwards our buildings shape us." This was true for my family; I felt we had been shaped by our houses. It was what Wright had wanted to do with Fallingwater as well, so "the most famous house in America" seemed like a perfect birthday present.

We flew into the Pittsburgh airport and bought a map of Pennsylvania that unfolded to a comically large fifteen square feet. As we were leaving the airport, my father was paged, a voice asking him to pick up a courtesy phone. It was my mother, calling to tell us that the bed and breakfast we had booked near Fallingwater was closed due to an unseasonal snowstorm that had felled trees and knocked out power lines. The whole area was without power. Fallingwater was closed as well.

My father put on a brave face, but he was deflated. He had planned our trip with his usual meticulousness, and now those plans were rendered useless before we even left the airport. We found a hotel in downtown Pittsburgh, ate lunch, then walked across the Andy Warhol Bridge and wandered the almost deserted Andy Warhol Museum, several floors dedicated to that industrious and bloodless Pittsburgh native, the homely boy who surrounded himself with beauty. Warhol wears the same expressionless expression in every photograph, standing with Jagger, Halston, Edie Sedgwick, et al. My father has the greatest natural curiosity of anyone I know and he was absorbed by Andy's world, but I was thinking: *What kind of birthday present is this?*

In the early evening we had a scotch in the hotel room and I browsed through Franklin Toker's *Fallingwater Rising*, a detailed account of the house. My father already knew all of the (sometimes apocryphal) anecdotes about its history and engineering. We finished our drink, then walked around quiet streets and picked a restaurant at random. Over dinner my father talked about the difficulties with Fallingwater's cantilevered balconies, which had sagged over the years and had had to be reinforced. He told me of Wright's life, which at times was operatically sorrowful.

Each father-son outing rides on a sense that the relationship will come to be defined by this football game or that fishing trip. When I turned thirteen, my father took me to

Hy's steakhouse for my birthday dinner, just the two of us, a rite of passage. I was dressed in a corduroy blazer and tie, a freckled hormonal volcano. As we were leaving for the restaurant, David, who was ten, picked up my birthday cake and pretended to throw it in my face, a Three Stooges joke, but as he held it cocked, his eyes wide in vaudevillian glee, it slid off the cardboard base and crumpled onto the floor. The plan had been to come home after dinner and blow the candles out and eat the cake. My name, written in icing in festive script at Jeanne's Bakery, disintegrated, and my brother burst into tears. We left my mother to deal with the situation and went to Hy's, a steakhouse filled with dark wood, cigarette smoke and salesmen's laughter. I was thrilled.

In Pittsburgh my father and I talked about David.

"I lost every argument with him," my father said.

He'd tried to steer David toward university, without luck. My father had gone to MIT on a scholarship and he and his two brothers were all professors. It was close to being a family business. My mother repeated the mantra that education was the key to success. But David felt he didn't need an education; his talent would sustain him.

My father recalled his parental warnings. "Do you want to be playing music in front of a bunch of drunks in a smoky bar when you're forty?" Now David was forty-eight and that was what he was doing, though it no longer sustained him.

My father had also lectured him on his pot smoking.

"You have a drink when you get home from work," David argued.

"But I don't have a drink when I wake up," my father had countered, adding that what he did was legal.

David's employment history was eccentric, but he'd recently gotten a job as the manager of the first Coles bookstore in Whitehorse, which made both my parents happy. He'd gone to Vancouver to take a managerial training course, and the store was set to open in a few weeks.

My sister and I were both relieved as well. We worried that he was becoming like a character out of a Raymond Carver story. Now we could imagine him up there, gainfully employed, secure.

The only one who wasn't relieved was David, though we had no way of knowing this at the time. While my father and I were talking optimistically about his new life, David was circling around the idea of his own death.

Frank Lloyd Wright was at a low point when he got the commission to design Fallingwater in 1934. He was sixty-seven years old and hadn't done a building in several years. His reputation was on the wane in America, exacerbated by the arrival of the Europeans and their Modernism. They were talking about internationalism and the house as a machine, and Wright's prairie sensibility suddenly seemed as quaint as a Winslow Homer painting. What infuriated Wright was the conviction that the Europeans had stolen their architecture from him, had taken the shapes and ideas in his work and bleached the humanity out of them, and then sold it as the future.

So when Edgar Kaufmann, a Pittsburgh department store owner, commissioned a weekend house from him, Wright had a lot at stake. He saw Fallingwater as a battleground that pitted him against all of Europe. The house in the Pennsylvania outback would be a monument. Plus the famously spendthrift Wright needed the money.

Kaufmann was a celebrated philanderer, his marriage a quiet ruin. He wasn't close to his son, Edgar Jr. As in most of Wright's houses, the bedrooms are tiny, only serviceable, and the central living space is the focus of the house, spacious, detailed and magnificent. Had Wright been designing for the Kaufmann family as it existed, he could have made three large bedrooms and a tiny communal area. But he tried to shape their world; he wanted to make it perfect.

My father had adopted the same philosophy for the house he designed for us. The bedrooms were small but the main floor was large and open, and the living room had floor-to-ceiling windows that were two storeys high. The hearth was at the centre, just as in many of Wright's homes. Dad was designing for the family he envisioned, the family we still were at that point.

The next morning started out crisp and blue, and my father and I decided we'd drive to Fallingwater anyway, just in case it reopened. Heading south out of Pittsburgh, we saw little evidence of a storm. There were a few small patches of snow on the hills, but the leaves were still on the trees, a faded pastel forest rolling across the Allegheny range. As clouds moved in, the landscape took on the grimmer look of *The Deer Hunter*, which had been set nearby, and the towns and hamlets had a tough, union, football-as-religion feel. As we got closer, there was still no sign of a storm. How could Fallingwater be closed?

We stopped at Kentuck Knob, one of Wright's last houses, built in 1954, five years before he died at the age of ninety-one. It was only a few miles from Fallingwater and contained many of his signature ideas, including what he called "client-proof furniture"—a built-in couch that ran the length of one wall. Almost everything in the house was designed by Wright, even the cutlery and plates. He created a universe; all you had to do was occupy it.

We bought postcards from the gift shop, and I noticed that one of the shots of the interior had a different configuration of the furniture that Wright had designed for the house. "Someone moved the furniture," I said to my father.

"That's probably what caused the storm."

Wildwood Park, where my brother and sister and I grew up, was a utopian urban plan that employed some of Frank Lloyd Wright's ideas about how environment could affect behaviour. One of his unrealized projects was Broadacre City, a work of social philosophy as much as architecture. Wright wasn't the only person searching for a better way for people to live. Two architects, Clarence Stein and Henry Wright, developed a residential model called Radburn at Fair Lawn, New Jersey. They called it "A Town for the Motor Age" and their design separated pedestrian and vehicular traffic. The houses fronted onto a huge common park.

The model was recreated in a handful of diverse places, among them Davis, California; Osaka, Japan; and Wildwood, where I grew up. The Wildwood houses were simple, essentially three designs with two slight variations, many of them clad in pastel-coloured, allegedly safe asbestos shingles. A vast park connected the houses, which meant we were protected from the outside world in a green and isolated Oz. Because the houses themselves were so mundane, little attention was paid to the development when it was constructed in 1948. Wildwood evolved into a cool enclave as people renovated their homes to match the clever setting.

Though my brother and I had no way of knowing this back then, we were living in the golden age of the North American middle class. The world (at least our corner of it) was affordable; our house had cost roughly what my father made in a year as an architect and professor (by contrast, my own modest Toronto house has a value more than twelve times my annual income). While there was still a breathtaking inequality between genders, among men there was a broad economic equality—American CEOs made twenty-four times what a worker made (that ratio is now 331 to 1).

The concept of upward mobility had currency; propping up the thriving middle class was a viable working class, many of whom, it seemed to me at the time, were involved in delivering things. We had a milkman who came to the door, and a breadman named Gord who arrived twice a week. My father's shirts were delivered in boxes with a paper band around them from Quinton's drycleaning in their distinctive green panel truck. Our doctor, a pragmatic Turk, came to our house when I had measles ("He'll live"). And every year, it seemed, something new arrived to make our lives better: colour TV; cumbersome, not very useful dishwashers that had to be attached to the kitchen tap; cable; polio vaccine (there were still a few kids in our school with either that distinctive limp or those steel bracketed polio crutches); power steering; the pill. And music, all that fabulous music. An explosion. That moment when rock and roll managed to be both innocent and subversive.

Within that Camelot-like historical blip, we lived in a neighbourhood that was what the suburbs could have been but rarely were. In the north end of my city there was poverty and misery, all of it unglimpsed by my brother and me.

Our family was a further honing of the middle-class dream. My father was handsome and well educated and a partner in a start-up architectural firm. My mother was beautiful and strong willed. They were both, by today's parental standards, absurdly young. They had met when my father came to Winnipeg to go to university. He boarded at my grandmother's house and fell in love with her red-haired daughter. Since she had other suitors, my father felt he'd better close the deal. They embraced a sleek modernist aesthetic, and we had cool Scandinavian furniture made of teak when most of our neighbours held to colonial maple dinette sets and overstuffed floral-patterned sofas, some of which had plastic covers on them. We had a hi-fi and jazz records, and there were ashtrays everywhere.

The immediate community seemed tight and effortless; whatever issues existed behind the identical doors—the alcoholism and depression and the undertow of madness that marked the end of the Age of Conformity—didn't become noticeable until much later.

When I was fourteen, we bought a big World War I–vintage house on a massive lot at the edge of the park, where we were still able to take advantage of Wildwood's charms. The elderly widow who had owned it was marrying the millionaire across the street (they were improbably named Mrs. Fox and Mr. Bird). The house was an anachronism—it had a coal-burning furnace, an ancient kitchen, worn linoleum and walls insulated with sawdust. It was incredibly dark. When my father and brother and I tore up the floorboards, we found newspapers from 1913 with crowded print and antiquated fonts and earnest ads for vinegar hair tonic. No one else had wanted to take on the challenge of this place, so we got it for a song.

My father redesigned the house completely, converting the garage to a mud room with an Italian tile floor and running a skylight across the peak of the roof to let light into those cloistered rooms. He knocked out walls and opened the main floor up into a flowing space. My brother and I were paid fifty cents an hour to unleash our destructive energies on the walls with hammers, smashing the plaster and lath. When the house was finished, it was a marvellous hybrid: part traditional prairie home, part modernist.

A photograph taken in front of that house shows the family in hopeful sixties fashions sitting among the fallen autumn leaves with our handsome, sweetly useless dog. My father has a hip, short-lived beard, and I am a tight-lipped adolescent, sullen and plotting rebellion. My sister, Alison, is still a perfect five-year-old, and between us is David, a blond-haired, blue-eyed, pudding-faced boy. My mother must have taken the picture because she isn't in it.

Most family photographs from any given era have certain similarities, posed and framed in the same way, wearing similar clothes, sporting the same haircuts and filmed with the same technology. When I see friends' old photos—the short hair, madras shirts, bare lawns, a Pontiac gleaming in the driveway—I'm struck by how interchangeable they seem. But with my own family photos, I see the context, I see what lurks outside the frame; the talents, limitations, antagonisms and kinship that bind us. I know the grown-up version of the innocent child, and I go through family photo albums with what Roland Barthes called "that rather terrible thing which is there in every photograph: the return of the dead."

The house is in the background of the photograph. It was unique, and it reinforced the idea that we were unique, coming out of an era of conformity, when individuality was slowly becoming prized in the colourful riptide of the sixties. The house was both reflection and affirmation.

My brother was a guileless child and completely open to the world. I was paralytically shy and used him as a buffer, getting him to ask directions, deal with adults, do anything that required interaction. He was a foil and a convenient target. One day when my mother was sewing, a rare thing, she asked where her pins had disappeared to.

"David swallowed them," I said, immediately and fictively.

"You *swallowed* them?" she said to David, who was standing next to her. He looked at me and nodded, a four-year-old along for the ride.

"Oh my god!" She loaded us into the front seat of our Corvair (only months away from being featured in Ralph Nader's screed, *Unsafe at Any Speed*, where it was described as a "one-car accident") and raced to the hospital. She had grabbed a loaf of bread on the way out the door and kept feeding slices to David, hoping the bread would cushion the trauma of the nonexistent pins. David chewed each piece of white, nutrition-free bread and then put the damp ball of dough into her purse as she careened toward the hospital, the three of us unbelted on the bench seat, sliding with every turn. Of course the X-ray showed no pins and the drive home was filled with probing questions and finally a tearful confession from the guilty party.

My brother and I had been closest when we were on family car trips. The back seat of our Corvair folded down (making it even less safe), and my mother put a blanket on it and we sprawled in the back, me reading, David bored because he couldn't read in moving cars or he would throw up, so he couldn't really do anything other than annoy me. I drew an invisible line down the middle of the seat marking territory that was inevitably encroached on—every time the car turned, we slid to one side or the other— which led to punches, which led to the car pulling over on the gravel shoulder in a cloud of dust and a lecture on harmony and the epic distances of the American Midwest.

Then Dad would set off again and we would lie down and watch the blue sky above the Black Hills of South Dakota go past. We stayed in motels with swimming pools and, since there was no one else to play with, we splashed and threw balls and played miniature golf on dinosaur-themed courses.

We sometimes drove to Minneapolis to see my uncle or to Fort Frances to swim in Rainy Lake. Left to ourselves my brother and I played board games, watched TV, invented games where I was heroic and he was villainous.

After years of modest, unairconditioned car trips, my parents splurged on a European vacation. I was fifteen, David was twelve, Alison six. In Geneva David suddenly disappeared. He was the kind of kid who wandered off, but it was one thing to disappear for a while in a small town, another in a foreign country. After a panicky search, we finally found him sitting at an outdoor café, arguing with a Swiss man about military conscription. We all sat down and had a coffee. The man mocked my brother's Prince Valiant haircut and said if he were his son, he would cut his hair and put him into the army.

"I don't want to kill anyone," David said.

———

Both my sister and I have a strong, somewhat romanticized attachment to our childhood environment. Alison lives a block from our old house in Winnipeg, in a modernist bungalow that is on a local architectural tour. As an adult, she still inhabits that happy geography.

I tried to recreate it in Toronto. At my insistence, my wife and I bought a house on a street that bordered a huge park, reminiscent of Wildwood. At the end of our street is the community hockey rink, almost exactly the same distance the rink had been from my house as a kid. I used to walk there in the dark on Saturday mornings and put on my skates in the players' box and practise by myself until first light, when other kids would arrive and a shinny game would form. The game went on all day, evolving as kids left and arrived, a mix of large and small, of talented and useless, of legendary puck hogs and local bullies. We played after the clubhouse closed at 7 p.m. and the lights were turned out, until Ronnie Walsh, the goaltender, got hit in the face with the puck and we took him home to his scary Irish mother. She had once leapt onto the ice during a game and clocked a kid on the other team.

"Playing in the dark, with a black puck," she said at the door as we delivered her bleeding son. "Bunch of geniuses, aren't you? Regular Einsteins."

"Yes, Mrs. Walsh."

"Don't give me any of your lip, you little bastards. And just look at my poor Ronnie."

On winter nights in my Toronto home I can hear pucks echoing off the boards, a sound I find comforting. On those nights when my wife feels we overpaid for the house, that the tens of thousands we spent on renovations failed to solve all its problems, that some other unseen, unbought house would have been perfect, absolutely perfect, she accuses me of having bought it in an expensive and misguided effort to recapture my childhood. And there are nights when I think she may be right.

But David, who hated to travel and hated the cold, went as far away from our childhood terrain as he could, seeking refuge at the ends of the earth. I wondered what he saw when he looked back on our perfect world.

My father and I drove to Fallingwater with the faint hope of good news, but the road was blocked and a uniformed woman with a walkie-talkie stood guard. She leaned into the window like a state trooper.

"You folks here for the Fallingwater tour?" she asked.

"Yes."

"It's going to reopen tomorrow: 9:30 a.m."

My father grasped her hand and said, "You don't know how happy this has made me."

I was filled with a profound relief. We booked tickets and found a hotel not far away, a big wooden building that looked like it might have once been a hunting lodge and had a giant steel swimming pool. A sign in the lobby noted that Johnny Weissmuller, the Olympic swimmer turned Tarzan, had swum there.

The next morning was cool, but the sun was out. We parked in the Fallingwater lot, then joined a group that walked down the path through the woods until those epic balconies came into sight and the house loomed like a mirage. We toured its rooms and paced the balconies, where a group of grade ten boys on a school outing were coordinating their jumps to see if they could make the balconies collapse. Beneath them, the famous waterfall flowed, the water moving under the house and spilling out with its trademark drama.

The guide gave us a circumspect version of the lives contained at Fallingwater. She didn't tell us about Edgar Sr.'s epic philandering. He once took a whole troupe of Ziegfeld girls to Atlantic City for the weekend. By the early 1950s, his mistress, who had the wonderfully Dickensian name of

Grace Stoops, was a regular fixture at Fallingwater. In September 1952, Edgar's wife Liliane committed suicide here, using sleeping pills. Edgar died three years later of bone cancer, shortly after marrying his mistress.

After the death of his parents, Edgar Jr. remade their family life into a harmonious unit set in that idyllic place. He renamed his mother's separate bedroom "the master bedroom" and called his father's bedroom the dressing room, implying a conjugal bliss they'd never achieved. His father had complained that Jr. had "refused to be a son," which may have been a veiled reference to his homosexuality. Certainly Edgar wasn't much of a father. But after his parents were gone, Edgar Jr. put a bust of himself on his father's desk and hung a portrait of the three of them on the wall. He removed Frida Kahlo's sexually charged paintings, perhaps a reminder of his father's libidinous nature. He studied architecture with Wright and wrote several books about Wright's work. Eventually, he donated Fallingwater to the Western Pennsylvania Conservancy. Over the years, hundreds of thousands of people have toured it, marvelling at its ingenuity and detail and its warm stone hearth. Amid the other Wright parishioners, my father and I took pictures of each other with Fallingwater in the background.

———

We flew out of Pittsburgh the next morning, back to Toronto. My father had a connecting flight to Calgary, and we embraced in the airport and said goodbye. I was grateful for the time together and for the fact that he'd gotten to see Fallingwater. It had been a wonderful trip.

A few weeks later my mother called. "Your brother has gone missing," she said.

3

A NORTHERN
MYSTERY

In late November, my brother didn't show up for his first day as manager of the bookstore in Whitehorse. He'd done his training, had physically set the store up. The staff was hired, the systems debugged. All that was left to do was to open the doors. But he didn't get there.

The next day, December 1, his truck was spotted at a rest stop on the Alaska Highway thirty kilometres south of town, beside the Marsh Lake Bridge that spans the Yukon River. A woman who used to work with him saw it and assumed it had broken down. But she noticed it was still there eight days later and reported it to the Royal Canadian Mounted Police, who drove out there and found the truck under a light dusting of snow, almost out of gas, unlocked, with the window rolled down. More ominously, they found David's cowboy hat sitting on the ground near the river. They got in touch with his wife Katherine, who phoned my parents.

That's when my mother called me in Toronto to say David was missing.

"Missing?

"He didn't show up for work, and he hasn't been home."

"How long has he been missing?"

"Ten days."

My first thought was that he'd fled his marriage and was off somewhere with a woman. The most likely spot was Vancouver. He'd just been there and perhaps he'd been seduced by its beauty. I was concerned, but I assumed he'd lit out, like in a country and western song. My mother and I tried to reassure one another that this was in character, that he'd be back. Though the timing was troubling. Why would he forfeit his new job at the bookstore? By the time I talked to my sister, later that day, I was worried. Wouldn't he have taken his truck if he was going to Vancouver?

The RCMP searched with dogs and an airplane, and might have searched the river but it was already half covered in ice. Dragging a river is both expensive and environmentally intrusive, and it isn't done much anymore. The North is filled with missing persons—people who have fled marriages, jobs, eastern complacency, the law, alimony payments and themselves. My brother was now officially one of them.

A week went by and no one in the family heard from him. In that grim lacuna between rumour and information, we waited. I phoned the Whitehorse RCMP, who had listed him as a missing person but hadn't ruled out suicide or "foul play," the quaint euphemism still used to cushion the blow.

I called Katherine and asked for the names and numbers of friends. She only gave me one, but with that I was able to find others. I didn't know any of them. I called a dozen people and assembled a daisy chain of anecdote and disbelief. A few thought he had staged his death and was living in Vancouver, or possibly Mexico. I called his doctor several times, but she didn't return my calls, probably because of privacy issues. David's health had never been brilliant—he had a tubercular cough from his lifetime of cigarette and pot smoking, a dreadful diet, and he never exercised. Maybe there was a dire health issue he hadn't told anyone about.

I tracked down the man who'd run the manager training session in Vancouver, who told me that David had done well, had enjoyed it. He was perplexed and said he hadn't seen any signs of a problem.

I constructed a timeline for David's last days. He checked into the River View Hotel on November 29 and was (allegedly) seen buying drugs that night. One friend noted he had a lot of cash on him; it turned out he had cashed his last two paycheques. Katherine told me she'd driven around town looking for him and saw his truck parked by the River View. She stopped and went in and found he was registered there and had prepaid with cash. She phoned his room from the lobby and a woman answered, then immediately hung up. Katherine didn't go to his room. Instead, she wrote a note and left it on the windshield of David's truck. She thought he'd be home in a day or so, contrite, seeking forgiveness.

I found a former bandmate named Ray who told me David didn't start drinking until the mid-nineties. David had taken the counterculture to heart and thought pot was hip, while drinking was something that Dean Martin did. But he jumped on the alcohol bandwagon in middle age.

A few years later, it was cocaine as well. "We were in the Bitter Creek Band at first, then just a duo," Ray said. "Played weddings. When his girlfriend left him, he was in a bad state and getting worse. His liver, I think. Went to the hospital in an ambulance. Doctor told him he had two to four years if he kept drinking. He was drinking on his lunch break at the radio station where he worked, beer and a shot. He also had a problem with girls. He cheated on Anna Mae, cheated on his wife, Katherine. It was the same as his drinking. Never enough."

Ray said there was a nasty faction in Whitehorse that hadn't always been there. "Seven, eight years ago, you knew everyone. There wasn't any violence." Ray didn't know what had happened to David, but like the RCMP, he hadn't ruled out foul play.

"He was very good at hiding his problem," he said. "A very good actor. He kind of had another life. He wasn't the guy I knew. He could sure play."

The portrait that emerged of my brother was filled with contradictions: he had habits that had grown over the last decade; he had been clean for two years; he was finally happy; he was desperately unhappy and feeling trapped. He was faithful, he had affairs, he was in debt.

As the days went by with no word from David, my family contemplated three scenarios. The most optimistic was that he had decided to start a new life. This, alas, was already the least likely, though some of his friends held to it; he was variously reported to have gone to Alaska, Vancouver and Mexico, where he was living the good life. The second was foul play, something that came up repeatedly in my conversations with his friends. The third was that he had taken his own life.

My father went to Whitehorse to look for him, staying at his house with Katherine. At that time of year there were less than six hours of daylight and the temperatures were frigid. He talked to the RCMP, talked to a few of David's friends and, after several dispiriting days, he returned.

My family held an unstated, faint hope that Christmas would bring some news. If he had simply taken off, surely he'd get in touch at Christmas. He would call our mother. But Christmas passed.

By then, the Yukon River had frozen solid; if my brother was in the water, we wouldn't know until spring. So we waited in our separate cities, my parents in Calgary, my sister in Winnipeg and I in Toronto.

I now believed that he had taken his own life. It was the most logical option, given the evidence. If he'd taken off, he would have gone in his truck, and he would have taken some of his instruments with him. If he had been murdered over a drug deal, as several people suggested, why leave the truck out there? It seemed too elaborate a misdirection, and there was no sign of a struggle at the scene. My parents and sister had quietly come to the same conclusion.

I went online, looking at suicide sites, reading the

literature. I decided to go up to Whitehorse and search for him myself, but it made sense to wait until the ice came off the river.

In the meantime, I kept calling his friends, trying to piece his life together. I tracked down David's last girlfriend, Anna Mae. They'd been together eight years. She was the girlfriend my mother thought was good for David, an enormously capable woman who could fix things, cook and was good with money. Anna Mae told me she had stood beside him for as long as she could, but she couldn't bear his infidelities and addictions. She finally left him, then left Whitehorse, moving to a semi-abandoned mining town in northern British Columbia. She told me that while David was engaged to Katherine, he had phoned her, asking her to take him back. Anna Mae sent him a letter, holding her ground; she said she loved him but couldn't go through all that again.

She sent me a copy of the letter, which was long and heartbreaking. "I know you don't want to be the way you are and do the things you do," she wrote to David. "But you have problems. They are your problems. I didn't cause them and I can't cure them. Only you can do that, if and when you are ready. It's like you're living two different lives. I hope one day you'll get the help you need. I believe you are a wonderful, caring, loving person, with problems. But those problems are too much for me to handle."

Anna Mae also told me that David had tried to commit suicide, a surprise. After she left him, he took sleeping pills and lay down on the couch in the basement. He left a note, saying he was leaving everything to his daughter, Ivy. He woke up, though, and crumpled up the note. When Anna Mae found out she called his doctor. He ended up in the hospital briefly.

I decided not to tell my parents this. I thought it would be better to wait until we had more definitive news about what had happened. My plan was to fly to Whitehorse in the spring, when the ice was off the river. I phoned the RCMP in April to find that the river was still frozen. May was no better. I finally flew to Whitehorse in the first week of June.

Whitehorse is just north of sixty degrees latitude, a city of twenty-eight thousand spread along the broad valley of the Yukon River and into the surrounding hills in pockets of suburban order. Though the plane arrived at midnight, the light still spread to the horizon with a benign glow, the moon sitting ghostly and superfluous in the western sky. The diurnal rhythm of the South is extended to seasons here, the long, dark winter followed by a relentless summer sun. The hills held ribbons of snow. Below me the Yukon River was wide and curving, a muted emerald green, carrying the detritus of spring down from the three mountains that flank the city.

It had been six months since David disappeared, but without the physical evidence my family didn't have any resolution. It occurred to me that we might never hear anything, that he had simply vanished from our lives. The act of moving here had been a vanishing act of sorts; Whitehorse is remote and expensive to get to.

David had originally come here with a woman who felt that the northern air would be good for her fragile health and that living in a small community might mitigate her agoraphobia; she turned out to be wrong on both counts and she eventually moved to Arizona.

At the time, he was recently divorced from Carolyn and looking for a change. For a while he and his girlfriend lived in a four-storey log cabin that had been divided into four one-bedroom apartments. It was a kind of fairy-tale building, where a troll or a wizard might live. She rarely left the apartment, spending her time nursing their pot plants and reading. David ventured out and returned late, bringing a version of the outside world home for her. It was ideal for him in a way: he roamed the town like a single man and returned each night to a stable relationship. But after a few years it fell apart, and she became part of the succession of wives and girlfriends who gave him motherly lectures on cigarettes, pot and his famously bad diet, which saw its first vegetable somewhere in the nineties. "I'm eating iceberg lettuce now," he once told me without too much irony.

David was spectacularly ill-suited to the Yukon. A lifelong indoorsman, he shunned sports and physical activity, was indifferent to the scenery, and had an almost pathological aversion to the cold. He liked heat the way very old people seek it, a musty, closed-window warmth that permeated his bones. He may have simply been looking for distance, though, and the Yukon is famous for it.

He got distance from me: this was only my second visit.

I had come up for his wedding two years earlier, along with my parents and my sister. The wedding was held in David's large, lovely backyard where Katherine stood on the back porch and sang Bette Midler's "The Rose" in an uncertain, determined voice. It wasn't a joyous event. David looked like a condemned man and said his vows with obvious irony. Katherine was a few years older than him, had taken his last name before the wedding, and was an endless source of New Age philosophy. (*Everything happens for a reason; you choose your own journey.*) She seemed to me to have taken my brother on as a project, arriving at a point in his life when his options were few and some part of him, surely, wanted to change. She hadn't lived in Whitehorse for long, and most of the people at the wedding were David's friends. Katherine told me Whitehorse was "the last place in the country you can be and do anything." She worked at the Wal-Mart. An hour later she said the town was a fishbowl; everyone knew what your business was. The marriage seemed to me to be a pragmatic union, for David the domestic equivalent of checking into a rehab facility.

At the reception that night, there was a jam session with a dozen musicians he'd played with at various times, David orchestrating everything, moving between instruments. He was so completely in control, and that mastery, those moments of musical harmony, must have felt wonderful. I still envied his gift.

One of his musician friends told me that there was an annual province-wide honky-tonk piano competition that David won three years in a row. They asked if he would judge the following year to give someone else a chance. He did; that year he entered the banjo-playing competition and won.

In deference to Katherine's wishes, the wedding reception was alcohol-free so it ended relatively early. The next day, my parents and sister and I toured Whitehorse and got a snapshot of David's world. At the airport, waiting for our respective flights home, my sister and I talked about the wedding.

"Can you say your vows ironically?" she asked. "I mean, even in the Age of Irony."

We reminisced about his first wedding, to Carolyn. It had also been held outdoors, by a creek behind our house with the Rocky Mountains gleaming in the background. It was the seventies and David was pony-tailed and stoned. Carolyn was radiant, surrounded by her lovely sisters, all of them looking like Klimt beauties in flowing dresses.

My sister and I tried to parse this new marriage.

"Well, he can't be alone," I said.

"Maybe Katherine will be good for him."

"In a prison guard kind of way."

Several friends had pointed out to us that the pair were codependent. Perhaps not the most romantic union, but middle age imposes compromise on many of us.

———

After the plane landed, I picked up my rental car at the airport and drove to the hotel. When I checked in, the woman behind the desk told me that they'd overbooked and could only accommodate me for the first three nights of my stay. I wasn't to worry, though: they'd found another hotel that could take me.

The blackout curtains in my room couldn't entirely keep the whiteness at bay, the light forming a glaring rectangle around the window. It was after midnight and I was tired, but knew I wouldn't sleep. I unpacked and went downstairs and walked the bright, quiet streets, weary though jangled. After an hour, I went back to my room and did a few exercises, then had an overpriced scotch from the mini-bar. I turned on the TV and flipped through the late-night graveyard: Barbara Stanwyck in black and white, up to no good, sitcoms, infomercials selling knives that cut through metal.

I lay down without much hope of sleep and drifted in and out, waking for good at 6 a.m. I dressed and walked to a café and ordered a melon-sized organic muffin and had two double espressos, waiting for the town to wake up. I had phoned ahead and booked interviews that morning with the RCMP and with a lawyer to talk about David's house, which was co-owned by my brother and

father and which Katherine apparently felt was now law-
fully hers.

Whitehorse was originally a meeting place for indigenous
peoples of the North. The Tutchone, Tagish and Tlingit
gathered here annually thousands of years ago to trade and
for the salmon run on the Yukon River. On August 16,
1896, two Tagish men—Skookum Jim Mason and Dawson
Charlie—found gold, and the resulting gold rush led
thousands of clerks to abandon their city lives down south
to wander in the snow, dreaming of riches.

The city still claims the residual spirit of the 1896
Klondike Gold Rush, but it became the territorial capital
in 1953 and is now essentially a government town, filled
with sturdy-legged bureaucrats, pioneers of a sort. The
Guinness World Records lists Whitehorse as the city with
the lowest levels of air pollution on the planet. It has a
curiously sprawled suburban layout with large gaps of
undeveloped land, as if the town planners were expecting
the core to grow at a rate that never materialized. People
still arrive with frontier dreams. On the streets, there were
winsome girls with Tibetan symbols tattooed on their
lower backs and young men with sun-scoured faces and

blond Rastafarian hair, stoner adventurers who were burning the days.

I was here to find out what I could about David, but I was also here to find a way to mourn. It isn't as easy as you'd think. When a friend of mine was diagnosed with terminal cancer and given a year to live, I began a quiet mourning while he was still alive, seeing him once a month at our regular poker game. The setting for the games got more elaborate: an expensive suite in a Toronto hotel, the casino in Niagara Falls, an artist's retreat. When he died, I wasn't as devastated as I thought I would be, perhaps because I had lived with his death for a year. He had been living with it himself, both on an existential level and on the pragmatic planes that death invites (making sure his family was taken care of, vowing not to drink any more cheap wine). His body was in the house for the wake, sitting in a comfortable chair. It sounds a bit macabre, though it wasn't. His physical presence made his death visceral; here was the proof. I sat there and looked at him and was overwhelmed, wishing that he would wake up and join the party. I had to leave and sat in my car sobbing.

Without David's body, I needed something else. A sense of his life up here at least. I needed to reconstruct the man I'd rarely seen in adulthood.

4

LONG DAY'S JOURNEY INTO NIGHT

I drove to the RCMP station and sat in the glum institutional waiting room amid glum locals. It couldn't be an easy town to police. Coke and meth and crack had all found their way here, bringing new addictions and violence.

After a few minutes, I was ushered in to see a short-haired, earnest officer who told me that a body had been found the previous week; it was someone who had gone into the river in December, but it wasn't my brother. He said they were expecting a few more people to surface. "The river gives up its secrets when it wants to," he said. They'd done an aerial search after the ice was off the river but hadn't seen anything.

I drove to the lawyer's office. She was a pleasant, sympathetic woman in her thirties. She told me that Katherine had taken out a caveat on the house, which meant she had expressed a legal interest in it, which would make it difficult if not impossible to sell. She walked me through the somewhat arcane ownership laws of the Yukon, laws that were further complicated by the fact that David wasn't legally dead. My father had been paying the mortgage on the house since David went missing, and my hope was that the house could be sold with some kind of amicable split of the proceeds that favoured my father and David's daughter (which is eventually what happened).

After I spent an hour going through the legal situation and my family's options with the lawyer, I drove to CHON-FM, the Indigenous radio station where David once worked, the only white person on staff. A friend of his at the station, Clint, told me he didn't think David was dead. "Those steps in the snow—he backtracked and left his hat and his truck," Clint said in a very quiet storyteller's voice. "Someone was waiting with a car. A woman. He might be in Alaska. Or maybe Vancouver."

As Clint spoke, I remembered David telling me about a television ad for a winter boot that was shot outside Whitehorse. The director had come to the radio station looking for someone to do a voiceover with a recognizably Indigenous voice. A few of the on-air people auditioned but weren't quite what the director wanted. When the man was leaving, David said, "I could do it, if you want."

A talented mimic, he read the script in the voice of a wise elder, the stereotype they were looking for, extolling the virtues of the boot in the extreme weather of the North. In a literal case of voice appropriation, David was hired for the ad. It ran for years, and at odd times while watching late-night TV, I'd suddenly hear his pitch-perfect imitation. "In my country. . ."

Clint had one of those voices where you just want to hear him talk. He told me that David would work late sometimes. "He wasn't in a rush to go home." He'd buy a six-pack and sit and quietly drink it at his desk.

I left the station and wandered the downtown, which is compact, everything within walking distance. I went into Mac's Fireweed Books and bought a few books on local history and the surrounding landscape. I stopped at the liquor store and picked up a bottle of wine and got a herbal sleep aid from a health food store, hoping one of them would help me sleep.

In the afternoon, I walked to the Blue Moon Saloon, where David used to play, a desolate building with a 1950s graphic of a couple dancing above the door. Outside, a small crowd lingered and smoked. They were lean and uncelebratory, heavily tattooed and partly bandaged. The men stood alone and the women huddled in small cliques. Inside, the air was sepia coloured. A group of men sat at a table with a woman. One of them had unbuttoned his shirt, and his heavy stomach rested on his belt buckle. His face was raw and vulnerable looking, as if someone had scraped a lemon zester across it. They were discussing ways of cooking a turkey over an open fire.

I introduced myself as David's brother to the manager, who didn't really know what to tell me. "Great musician," she said, nodding vigorously.

David had played here hundreds of nights, on a stage that sits above a pit containing a dozen tables. I remembered bars like this when I went to university, dives on the east side of Calgary that held a sleazy charm for students. They were cheap and colourful and, we felt at the time, authentic in some way. But whatever romance they held only worked if you didn't spend your days draped over a table sipping draft beer, talking about ancient slights and heroics, and your nights in a flophouse.

I had gone to see David in the King Edward Hotel in east Calgary, and he remained drawn to such places. When the family got together in Calgary, he would disappear in the evening to drink at the Cecil, a rundown bar on the east side. Occasionally he'd sit in with the band.

After chatting with the manager, I went into the small

off-sales room attached to the bar, where I knew a friend of David's named Adeline worked. A few people drifted in and bought beer and gin and cigarettes as we talked. Not everyone paid, I noticed, though she kept track of their tabs.

"It was foul play," she told me, speaking *sotto voce* even though there was no one else in the store. David had developed a cocaine habit in the 1990s, Adeline said, and she had watched it progress. There was a drug dealer, a man in a wheelchair with a mean streak, who sometimes sold to him. She let this hang, but the implication was that this guy could have harmed David.

She told me that between sets at the Blue Moon, David would go down to the Yukon River, which is only two blocks away, walk across a narrow-gauge railway track that used to carry supplies during the Klondike Gold Rush, and clamber down a small scree bank to a rim of sand along the water. He would bring a few Corona beers, a joint and a woman, and sit near the river. A refuge of sorts.

"I could tell which woman he was with by the brand of cigarettes he bought," she said.

Adeline saw David on November 30 when he popped in to say hello. He didn't buy anything. He was in a good mood. He told her he was headed to The 98, a popular spot for drug deals, the *ultima Thule* of dives. After that, no one saw him.

Adeline's knowledge of the local drug world was filled with generalities and foreboding and, despite my prodding, was short on specifics. She regarded me, rightly, as a nosy outsider. She felt David might have been killed by someone in the drug world, though he had been pretty clean for a while. Maybe he'd gone with a woman and she told someone he had money, Adeline said ominously. Told the wrong guy.

"I'm guessing this town has a few wrong guys," I said.

"Filled," she said. "Filled."

My brother and I were opposites in so many ways, and my mother's parenting strategies had the unintended effect of pushing us farther apart. She limited the amount of television we could watch to ten hours a week, which seems wildly restrictive in a modern context, but back in the three-channel (one of them in French), black and white, manually-adjusting-the-antenna-for-better-reception era, you could barely find ten hours of decent programs a week. We watched *The Ed Sullivan Show*, *Gilligan's Island*, *The Man from U.N.C.L.E.* and *Mission: Impossible* and still had six and a half hours to spare for cartoons (though she briefly banned Bugs Bunny for being too violent, because of all those characters getting whacked with mallets or blasted with shotguns). But my mother didn't always keep track, and we could watch at friends' houses. I have been indifferent to television all my life. My brother, on the other hand, grew into a TV addict. He watched endlessly and had an extensive video collection of movies and television series. He had hundreds of plots and characters and accents in his head and often quoted from shows, did little routines.

When we were kids our mother didn't allow soft drinks in the house. As with guns and television, she led a singular, unappreciated charge against sugar that was ahead of its time. In an era when every kid on the block was swimming in Orange Crush (when doctors had only recently stopped recommending Camel cigarettes in magazine ads), she wouldn't buy soft drinks. We could drink root beer in frosted mugs when we went to the A&W, and we could have soft drinks when we went on car trips to the United States. We would stop in small-town general stores that had red steel coolers and lift that lid to see unfamiliar brands sitting in icy water. We each got to pick one, and we treasured those Fantas and cream sodas. As I grew up I lost all interest in soft drinks. As an adult, David started each day with a half-litre of Pepsi in place of coffee, and he drank it all day.

As a child, David's sweet tooth was an addict's. He ate raw white sugar by the tablespoonful. When his supply was cut off at home, my mother placing anything sugary out of reach, he appealed to neighbouring mothers, going door to door asking for cookies or candies. For a while, my mother hung a sign on him that read, "Please Don't Feed the Sugar Pig."

Faced with a piece of cake, David would eat the icing first, then stare at the unadorned cake, while I would skilfully eat the cake and leave the icing standing, two parallel vertical lines of sugar and butter connected by the thick horizontal line. Our plates were perfectly complementary. He wanted my icing, of course. He tried stealing it with his fork, which I easily parried, then he'd cry and my parents would deliver a lecture on how balance was important in life. Oddly, his sweet tooth for anything other than Pepsi disappeared as he grew up, while I developed a late-onset chocolate jones. It was as if he left this particular addiction in my care after he'd moved on to other things. Suddenly I was eating five Kit Kat bars a day with the same mechanical joy that smokers bring to their fortieth cigarette.

I loved sports and played incessantly as a kid; he shunned

them. I read avidly; he preferred television. I was musically ungifted; he had that remarkable talent.

When our parents dutifully enrolled us in Cub Scouts, a troop that met in the basement of the United Church, I adapted quickly to the bullying British army environment, while David quit after a few months, declaring that it was a Hitler Youth organization. He was ten. So he missed the knots and badges, the chants of allegiance to Akela, and the sight of a fellow cub's front teeth skittering along the hardwood floor of the church basement when he was tackled in a game of British bulldog that got out of hand.

David was a social man, had been a social boy. I was a happy, socially integrated kid, but I was naturally shy and sought solitude, a habit that mushroomed in adulthood. He never lived alone. He moved out of our parents' house into his first wife's house. Within a few days of his eventual divorce, he was living with another woman. He was never without a girlfriend, and along with those girlfriends, there were dozens of affairs. Except when he was driving around in his truck, he was almost never by himself.

In our house west of Calgary, there was a separate furnace and thermostat for the ground floor, where all the kids' bedrooms were. David was in the warmest bedroom, nestled into the hill, partly below grade. I was in the coldest—which was cantilevered over a ravine, and the underinsulated floor was like a skating rink. But I craved cold. I was brilliantly adapted to the frigid prairie winters we experienced as kids, where my outdoor hockey games were cancelled only if it was colder than −25°F *with a north wind,* a caveat that spoke to the local attitude to weather.

On winter nights, David would pad down the hallway and turn up the thermostat to a ridiculous temperature, where the furnace would be working most of the night. I would get up and turn it down. He'd get up and turn it to its highest setting; I'd turn it off completely. Victory went to whoever stayed awake the longest. Arctic or Sahara—we rarely found a happy medium.

Finally, my brother and I looked different, bearing only a passing family resemblance. But in certain disturbing ways, we weren't so different. And in Whitehorse, I found traces of David that were uncomfortably familiar.

The relentless daylight already felt oppressive. I had a heavy pasta dinner and three glasses of wine, with the thought that this would help me sleep. I walked back to my hotel and undressed, and lay down and stared at the ceiling. I thought about my father coming up here in that brutal cold, a seventy-five-year-old man looking for a lost son in the endless night. The idea of him making these same rounds was heartbreaking.

I turned on the television and watched five minutes of a fishing show, then sat through a film noir caper starring Sterling Hayden. At 4 a.m. I finally got dressed. Outside, the streets were almost empty and the light had a velocity, as if we were roaring toward a brightness no one could bear.

There were bloodstains and cigarette butts on the sidewalk outside Lizards Lounge, as if two men had had a fight, then spent a long time discussing it. The pale moon sat in the western sky. A few clouds gathered on the horizon. Down by the river, three men were drinking beer. I had the sense that most of the bad things that happen at night had already happened.

In the windows of government buildings, there were energetic poster campaigns to reduce fetal alcohol syndrome, to respect elders, to quit smoking, to not drive under the influence of pot, to avoid, whenever possible, divorce.

I walked around thinking of David. He was a night person, staying out late and sleeping late. He could be one of the restless citizens still prowling in the endless dawn, one of the guys by the river drinking beer and smoking cigarettes, without the darkness to insulate them. All the acts that night was created for—drug deals, affairs, theft—were conducted here in the flashbulb of noon. David was a night person in a place with no night for part of the year. Perhaps it was the Whitehorse winter he loved, in spite of the cold—that unending night.

David had come to alcohol late in life, but it gradually became another addiction. Those of us who lean toward the French in our alcohol consumption (two or three glasses of heart-sustaining red wine per day), who long ago quit smoking, who occasionally smoke the odd joint more out of nostalgia (and are ambushed by its alarming potency) are aware of how little separates us from the addicts. In middle age, I had several friends who had had to quit everything, who woke up one day to interventions or domestic calamity or severe health warnings. It isn't hard to quietly stagger into the clinical. One day you're a social drinker, the next day you're alone with your habit, then alone with your addiction. A friend told me that it wasn't drinking at parties that was the problem, it was drinking alone in his basement. So much about middle age is the toll of small things adding up (I should have flossed more, taken up yoga earlier, put more money aside).

Our habits require vigilance. At least mine do. Every January I abstain—no alcohol, chocolate or caffeine. I don't always make it through the entire month. I do it less for health reasons than to prove to myself that I can. A friend of mine abstains from New Year's to Easter, then pours himself a hearty single malt. I haven't slipped into addiction as my brother did, but I know its subtle pull. Our habits are like gardens; they need maintenance, pruning. You need to tear out the weeds or it all goes to hell. Unsurprisingly, addiction is a statistical marker for suicide.

At 6 a.m. the streets were empty, the sky without colour. I went back to the hotel and retrieved the book I'd bought about local flora and fauna, then went to the same café and had three espressos and another giant muffin. I leafed through the book, learning that this far north, the rate of natural decay lessens. There are fewer organisms at work. Those armies of earthworms and beetles and bacteria in the south are reduced to sentries up here. Eight months of dark winter are too much for most life.

5

DINNER AT THE END OF THE WORLD

I called David's wife Katherine, and we agreed to meet for dinner that night. At 6 p.m. I picked her and Adeline up and we went to a restaurant. Katherine delivered a lengthy monologue that described her own heroic journey and how the whole community looked to her as a noble example of something.

A former bandmate had told me that Katherine had helped David, and as a result he felt he owed her. Here was the essential dilemma, he said: David could be the man she wanted him to be (gainfully employed, at home in the evening, sober) or he could be the musician he longed to be. She wanted him to stop playing, to stop going on the road, and get a job in town. One reason she didn't want him on the road was that that was where his appetites went unchecked. Though perhaps some part of him wanted respite from those too. I once asked a friend of mine who had quit drinking if it had been difficult. "It was a relief," he said.

Katherine told me they wanted to set up a foundation in David's name that helped local musicians. "We've gotten pledges for between a hundred and a hundred and fifty grand," she said. "For the foundation."

This seemed wildly unlikely, but I didn't pursue it. I wondered if she and Adeline were about to ask me for a donation.

I asked them about David's drinking, about drugs.

"I got him to quit drinking," Katherine said. "He wasn't doing drugs."

Adeline nodded, though she had a slightly different version. "He had a problem," she said. "He was trying to quit but, you know, he had gotten into a crowd. With music he was always alive. But with the drugs, sometimes you could tell he was gone by the second set. Whatever happened to him, he didn't expect that moment."

We chatted about David for a while, then after dinner we drove out to the Marsh Lake Bridge where David had stepped into the water. I stopped for gas and was surprised when the gas station wouldn't accept my credit card. I phoned the number on the back and a woman answered. I asked her why my card had been refused.

"We thought the card might be stolen," she said. "We didn't think it was you."

"Why wouldn't it be me?"

"Well, way up there, up north. Is it cold? What are you doing up there, anyway?"

"Looking for my brother."

"Well, I sure hope you find him!" she said cheerily and unblocked my card.

We drove along the unpopulated highway, the washed-out sky fading further behind the mountains.

"I need to keep that house," Katherine finally said, staring straight ahead. She told me she didn't know how the mortgage was being paid.

"My father's been paying it." I suggested she talk to a lawyer, though I knew she'd already seen one.

"I talked to a lawyer," she said, "but not for anything legal."

I decided not to pursue this contradiction.

At the bridge we got out and walked. Swallows were nested on the bridge supports and poplars grew along the banks. An eagle flew over, and Katherine said it was most likely David's spirit. We stood in silence for a while, staring at the river, then Katherine said, "David always thought he was a blemish on the family."

That was a heartbreaking thought. He had always been an outlier. My parents, my sister and I all had birthdays in the first weeks of September, but David was stranded in May. Physically, he looked different than we did, the only blond in the family. He was a black sheep, though I had thought it was by design. Now I wasn't so sure.

I remembered a Sunday from childhood, getting ready for church, sitting in the wooden pew with our grandmother, David fidgeting, my grandmother placing a calming hand on him. Afterwards we went to her house. David and I sat in her backyard, each with a cup of white sugar, dipping rhubarb from her garden into it and taking a bite. A reward for coming to Jesus. My great-uncle Jim came by in his spotless two-tone Chrysler Imperial. It was said that he had money. Jewel your crown, my grandmother would tell us cryptically in reference to him. He offered to give David and me a ride in his fancy car. Jim was dapper and eccentric and epically thrifty. He didn't like to stop at red lights, as it wasted gas. We sat in the back seat and Jim hardly said a word. A prairie thunderstorm was approaching, the sky bruised in the west. We drifted through red lights—the traffic sparse, Sunday still a day of rest back then. We sat like hostages in our blazers, watching the city go by in the plush silence of Jim's Imperial. David had granules of white sugar stuck to his face. When we got back to my grandmother's, Jim didn't come to a full stop, fearful of wasting gas. David and I spilled out onto the curb and stumbled onto the grass, and Jim sailed away. We lay on our backs in our Sunday clothes for a moment, staring at the darkening sky. Everything still a mystery.

David's walk along the December ice to the open water would have been about twenty metres. I stood there imagining that walk, compulsively running through what I thought had happened, tears arriving. David had driven down the Alaska Highway, tired, buzzing. I knew that he had been listening to a cassette of his first band in his truck, a twenty-year-old recording. He had apparently been playing it for two weeks. When he pulled over at the scenic stop, he rolled down the window, took the Nytol he'd brought and lit a cigarette, and sat there smoking until the gas gauge read empty. Perhaps what came to him wasn't a series of rational thoughts but a blunt yearning that pulled like an undertow. He wanted to be unburdened. The darkness and pain that he'd kept at bay filled him and he was spurred by the impassive December cold. The sleeping pills made him sluggish. He got out of the truck, placed his hat on the ground and walked to the open water.

I hoped that some peace descended on him as he stood there, so alone. The blue-eyed boy who loved music.

We drove back, our conversation exhausted, and I dropped Katherine and Adeline off where Katherine had left her car. I went to my hotel and once again was unable to sleep. I adjusted the curtains, flipped through television channels, read a bit, stared at the ceiling, thought about David. I'd spoken to a former bandmate of his named Gary who had been playing with him for the last two years. Gary had never seen him do drugs or drink. His only bad habit was cigarettes. Onstage, he said, David was calm. There was a lot he didn't know about David, Gary told me.

I drifted off to sleep toward morning. When I awoke, I was suddenly panicked, afraid I'd slept until noon, but it was just past seven. I was jittery and raw and went back to the same café to order the same muffin and espresso.

After breakfast I went to David's bank. Near the end of November, his bank account was overdrawn and he owed money on two credit cards. His last mortgage payment hadn't been made by him.

I walked to the off-sales at the Blue Moon to chat with Adeline again, to see if she would give me more information about David's contacts with any drug dealers. While we talked, Katherine came in. She was crying. "David was pulled out of the water," she said. "He's at the coroner's."

I felt stunned. It wasn't as if I'd held out any real hope he was still alive, but now he was irrefutably gone. The news shouldn't have been a surprise, yet it was and I felt hollowed by it.

I went back to my room and called the coroner. I wanted to make sure it was David before I called my parents. As it turned out, just hours after I arrived in Whitehorse, a jogger saw his body near the shore of Schwatka Lake and called the RCMP, who came and pulled him out. I wondered if the RCMP officer was aware of this when I was in his office; perhaps David had been discovered but they didn't have a positive identification. I asked the coroner how she'd identified him.

"He fits the description," she said. "And there's a tattoo, a bird, on his chest." An osprey—the name of one of his first bands. After almost six months in the water, he had travelled thirty kilometres down the Yukon River into the lake that is formed by the hydro dam just outside of Whitehorse. They were going to ship his body to Vancouver to perform an autopsy.

I asked the coroner about coming in to make a positive identification of David. Just to be absolutely sure.

"Well, I don't know that you want to do that," she said.

"No?"

"Well, I mean, he travelled thirty kilometres along the river. The thing is, you have to decide how you want to remember him. Because you probably won't get this image out of your mind. It's your decision. I'm just saying."

I thought about it for an hour. The coroner was right; whatever I saw lying there I wouldn't be able to unsee. I decided to take her advice.

I called my parents and my mother answered.

"They found David," I said. "He was pulled out of the water three days ago, but they just told me now."

"It's him?"

"The osprey tattoo."

"Ohhhh."

My mother wailed. She'd known, we all had. Still, here it was, finally, the proof. Dad was on the other line, silent, stunned. I didn't know what else to say except that I'd try and wrap up his affairs as best I could. We decided on cremation; we could spread his ashes somewhere he'd been happy. We didn't want him buried in this cold ground so far away from us.

————

When I tried to imagine my mother's grief, I had to think, reluctantly, of my own children. My daughter, Justine, had been a colicky baby and often woke up crying, inconsolable. Most nights my wife would get up and breastfeed her in the hope that that would work. Occasionally I would roll out of bed and try to calm her. I would hold her and walk in small circles and move in that baby-jostling rhythm that seems innate to every parent, and softly sing a medley of Johnny Cash songs ("Ring of Fire," "Folsom Prison Blues," "I Walk the Line") in my best imitation of his basso voice. Miraculously, it sometimes worked. I wondered if it was simple biology, a reaction to that deep voice—that whoever was attached to it would protect her forever.

We can't protect them forever, of course. But parenthood is made up of thousands of these moments—something visceral in the dark when you are pressed against your child with your secret thoughts. My mother had experienced all those moments with David, and they still sat inside her, but now they were all she had.

My mother's hopes and expectations for her children were outsized. She gave both David and me subscriptions to the *Guardian* to broaden our minds. When I moved to Toronto to become a writer and was working as a busboy in a failing restaurant, I would get letters from my mother that had employment opportunities attached; Oxford was looking for a new chair for their English department, or there was an opening in the diplomatic corps coming up. My brother would have been getting something similar.

Most parents have these hopes and we adjust as we go. My mother had recalibrated her expectations, had remained hopeful and loving and had appreciated David's gifts and understood his limitations.

When a police officer came to our door one Sunday morning after some friends and I had been nabbed the previous night drunkenly trying to pull a stop sign out of the ground, my mother burst into tears and actually said the words, *Where did we go wrong?*

She didn't go wrong, though occasionally we did. Parenting is inexact and perilous and designed so you can't solve every problem. The rewards of parenthood are many, but the grief is bottomless.

Katherine held an impromptu dinner that night. Friends of David's were there, some of whom I'd talked to already but many of whom I hadn't met. Katherine had insisted that under her careful supervision David hadn't had a drink or any drugs in more than a year, and that he was faithful.

A bandmate told me he was regularly getting high and sleeping with whomever he could. Another musician said it was hard to tell with David because he could play drunk and sound sober, but that he'd seen him drinking.

All of these versions of David were sitting at the dinner table as we chatted about him. There were ten of us, including Clint, whom I'd spoken to at the radio station. He was filled with grief; he'd held on to the idea that David was alive and happy and living somewhere warm, and was devastated to be confronted with the truth.

A woman named Roxanne who had worked with David in radio told me how generous he was, how he had helped so many in the community. He lent people money, drove them where they needed to go. She was lovely and graceful and said there had been a connection between them that hadn't quite gelled into romance.

The combination of grief, sleep deprivation and wine made me feel disembodied. In conversation, I felt like I was both talking and watching a scene unfold from above. My prefrontal cortex was working overtime, processing information a second late, everything on a tape delay.

I went downstairs to use the bathroom. The house was a split-level and David's world was down here. There was a television and all of his instruments—guitars, banjo, mandolin, electric bass, harmonicas—and his vast store of books, records, CDs, DVDs and videotapes. He had recreated this space in several houses, inhabiting each one with his barking laughter, smoker's cough and demons.

I could see David in this room, playing the banjo, his fingers flying over the fretboard. On a table, there was a plastic bag that Katherine had picked up from the coroner that contained the contents of his pockets—a cigarette case, a gold pocket watch that had suffered some damage, two five-dollar bills, a cheque for a hundred dollars and a mortgage statement. I took the watch out and examined it. He often wore a vest and kept the watch in one of its pockets, checking it for the time like a nineteenth-century stationmaster.

His instruments were lined up, guitars on stands or in cases. I wanted to have something of his—and what better than a banjo or guitar, something he'd held onto for so much of his life. I remembered taking our musical theory exam at the university downtown when we were kids. He finished quickly, then sat waiting for me. Afterwards we walked to a nearby department store and bought cream puffs in the bakery in the basement. They were on sale, likely a day old, soggy and defeated. We ate one each, then went to the top floor of the parkade with the idea of dropping the remaining two on the people waiting at the bus stop below.

"You don't have to throw them, just drop them," I said.

"Why do *I* have to drop them?"

"You're saying you don't even know how to drop a cream puff?"

"I know how. But why does it have to be me?"

"You have to learn sometime." As if this was a marketable skill.

He leaned against the railing, holding the two cream puffs, an innocent. He let them go and we hightailed it out of there, rattling down the urine-smelling stairwell. In our minds, the cream puffs had landed with nuclear impact and when we strolled nonchalantly by the bus stop, having an animated conversation about something, we would witness cream spread out in a kill zone that extended to ten feet. But there was no trace of anything. No wailing cream-covered citizens staring upward, no trace on the sidewalk. How can you miss *everything*?

As an adult, David helped me learn to play the guitar. After I had mastered a few chords, he recorded me singing and playing an awful song I co-wrote, titled "You're My Test Tube Baby" ("Test Tube Baby, science made her . . ."). He had the patient air of an older brother, adjusting microphones and levels, having me try a key that was less anguished to sing in, giving me a glimpse of the natural musical leadership that flowered in his various bands. He was generous with me, in part because there wasn't any competition between us in the realm of music. We had staked out separate territory in almost everything, so there was little direct competition anywhere.

Oddly, as an adolescent, I had briefly been part of a band, on piano, of all things. I could play one song, The Monkees' "Last Train to Clarksville." The other members knew a second song, the instrumental "Wipe Out." No one could sing. We were offered the chance to play at the local community centre dance, and we had a band meeting to ponder this gig as if we were the Beatles contemplating Shea Stadium.

In David's basement, I was suddenly tempted to pick up one of his guitars and play one of the two songs I remembered ("Sweet Virginia" by the Rolling Stones, and Ian and Sylvia's "Four Strong Winds"). But there were musicians above me.

I don't know how long I stayed down there. When I came upstairs, Clint was getting ready to leave. David's friends continued to be earnest and helpful, but we didn't know what we wanted or needed from one another. We exchanged stories; I offered up the child and they responded with the adult. We lingered over our wine and listened to David's music and the evening went by.

I went back to my hotel room. The rectangle of light around the blackout curtain plagued me. It was the kind of light you see in science fiction movies—one that suggests a powerful malevolent force only barely held at bay. Lying on the bed, the wine souring in my head, I turned on the television and listlessly watched five minutes of six different shows.

David and I had been most allied in mischief. I remembered the two of us buying fireworks one summer when we were kids in Fort Frances. I'm twelve, and our twelve-year-old cousin Peter, nine-year-old David and I walked across the bridge from Fort Frances to International Falls, Minnesota (birthplace of celebrated make-up artist Tammy Faye Bakker) to buy fireworks, which were more inventive and destructive in the United States. We came back with a box that held enough gunpowder to blow a bank vault, waved through by a smiling border guard.

Instead of a bank, we used the fireworks to blow up the garden at the cottage my parents were renting. In that spectacular gap that exists between action and consequence for twelve-year-olds, we saw it as a victimless crime. Among the fireworks were several packages of blockbusters, almost dynamite-like, which had a violent effect in the garden. When my parents returned and saw the Dresden-like damage—the hydrangeas levelled, the violets and daisies obliterated, the roses blackened and crippled—they were furious. The cottage belonged to a childhood friend of my father's.

"This was Annie's garden," my mother said.

That was going to be our defence—it was just a garden.

"She spent days—weeks—planting it, taking care of it. You've destroyed it. What do have to say for yourselves?"

We wished we'd blown up someone else's garden. "We're sorry."

"Do you know how much *time* she put into that garden? How much it meant to her? Do you?"

We didn't. We didn't really grasp much past our narrow worlds. We lacked awareness, as my mother emphasized. We were in the last throes of childhood, before puberty arrived with its confusion and guilt. We were made to apologize to Annie. And we all had to leave the cottage. In the car, my mother stared wistfully out the window and said, "We can never go back."

When we went to Europe on our grand tour, my parents sometimes went for dinner on their own. I was fifteen, left in charge of the twelve-year-old David and our six-year-old sister. In Venice we sat in our sort-of grand hotel, which had a lot of marble, and listened to gondoliers singing corny songs for tourists as they poled by in the canal below. David had bought balloons for some reason, and we filled them with water and threw them at the gondoliers from the hotel window. We missed repeatedly, but finally connected with one of our last two balloons. A gondolier with an exaggerated tenor was belting out Tom Jones's "Delilah" below us, and we each let one go and ducked behind the balcony wall to hear the song stop abruptly, followed by an impressive stream of Italian curses. Our guilty hysteria was accompanied by the spectre of Italian police breaking down the door.

What are we anchored by? David was anchored by his talent, certainly, but I think it was less of a comfort than it had been, that it had grown into something like a reflex. His family was dispersed across the country. He saw his daughter when he could, though Ivy spent more time with my parents than with David. He had once been the colourful sibling, dressed in cowboy boots and cowboy hat, his hands restless and jangling as if they needed to be connected to an instrument. A series of small steps that began years ago had finally brought him to a landscape he couldn't bear.

6

SOLO CANOE

Mornings don't arrive here. Instead there is a soft expansion of light, barely noticeable. I had slept for two hours or so, not consecutively. Perhaps another hour in that half-awake state where you dimly acknowledge the illegitimacy of your dreams, aware that Penélope Cruz isn't sitting in the faded wing chair happily picking at a room service breakfast.

The day I'd arrived, I had booked a canoe at a local outfitter. My idea had been to paddle down the Yukon River and look for David, despite the wild unlikelihood that I would find him. Now that he had surfaced, I decided to go down the river anyway. I got dressed and went back to the familiar café. My ongoing sleeplessness made surfaces shimmer slightly. The air was sharp. Every noise seemed amplified, and my peripheral vision picked up movements that may not have been there. A man came into the café, under five feet, tanned the colour of black tea, bald, walking with a pugnacious hunch, as if anticipating a fight, wearing dancer's slippers. He looked like something from Middle Earth. It wasn't immediately clear that he was real.

I collected my order from the counter, then went to pick up my canoe. The outfitter, a ruddy-cheeked outdoorsman, asked me about my canoeing experience (quite a bit, but long in the past), and I asked about the river, whether there were rapids or anything else I should know. How long would it take to canoe back to town from the Marsh Lake Bridge?

"Back before you know it," the man said. "Piece of cake." He gave me the coordinates for a shack on the bank of the Yukon River that belonged to a bush pilot. I could use the phone there and someone would come and get me and drive me to my car.

We strapped the canoe to the roof of my car, and I drove to the bridge. Two-toned recreational vehicles with names like Zephyr and Ulysses driven by retirees moved in small convoys. In December this road would have been sparsely travelled and dark by early afternoon.

I arrived at the bridge and parked and put the canoe in and drifted slowly downstream. It was warm, 22°C, though the breeze held a coolness, a reminder there was still snow in the hills, that the ice had come off the river only a few weeks ago. There was enough wind to keep the mosquitoes away, though the water was calm. The river was wide, cutting through sandbanks crowned by ridges of pine. The mountains in the background were obscured by cloud. The water was as placid as a pre-dawn lake, and at a hairpin turn it mirrored the twenty-five-metre cliff with such eerie precision it was like entering a special effect. There were dead grey pines in marshy shallows near the shore. No one else was on the water.

There is a specific peace that comes with solo canoeing when the only sound is your paddle dipping into the water, as rhythmic as breath. I'd canoed a lot when I was young, starting at summer camp. At fourteen, I went on a two-week trip organized by the camp, paddling through the pristine wilderness of northern Ontario. I almost drowned on that trip. On a portage, I was carrying the ninety-pound food pack, still mostly cans in those days. It was the heaviest pack, but as the trip guide pointed out, it got lighter every day. Those who chose the forty-pound packs had a uniform burden, but mine would lighten and ultimately vanish. But at this point it was still too heavy for me to get on by myself, and I staggered under its weight. We were portaging through a stretch of thick forest, walking along a stream, as it was the easiest path. The stream wasn't deep. I was walking at the back. I slipped on some rocks and fell backward into the water. I was pinned by the weight of the pack behind me, completely submersed. The air was only a few inches away, the forest canopy distorted slightly by the moving water. I twisted to try and turn over, but the pack was too heavy. I couldn't get up. I tried to wriggle out of the straps, but they were cinched tight and I didn't have any leverage. The trip guide looked behind him to see one of my hands sticking out of the water and rushed back. He wasn't much older than I was, perhaps eighteen. He pulled me up with difficulty. "What the hell were you doing?" he yelled into my face. Drowning.

A week into the trip we had to do a three-day solo, each of us dropped on a separate small island with a square of baking chocolate, a half-cup of oats and a package of dehydrated soup. We had a knife, matches, a tin pot, our sleeping bag and ground sheet, and a fishing line with a hook. Make a fire, catch a fish, find berries, make sure they aren't poisonous. See you in three days, men.

I sat on a rock and tried to catch a fish, my line baited with a leech. There weren't any fish. Or any berries. The solitude was spectacular. It had breadth and depth and height. The night sky was mammoth. The first evening the mosquitoes were so loud, I thought a motorboat was approaching. I built a fire and sat in the smoke, then sought refuge in my sleeping bag. The torment they provided was biblical. While I liked solitude, I had never been alone like this. I hadn't lived enough to spend three days contemplating life. Discovery, awe and misery mingled in complicated layers. At the end of those three impossibly long days, the trip guide picked me up first. He had two canoes tied behind his, and we stopped and picked up the others. We returned to our base camp and gorged ourselves, suspecting that the three-day solo had been an impromptu way of dealing with the fact that the organizers hadn't brought enough food for two weeks. We told each other stories of unsuccessful fishing, of mosquitoes and bears. No one spoke of the solitude because we didn't know how.

Ahead of me on the river, I spotted two canoes roped together, moving slowly. Swallows darted along the surface of the water in graceful swerves. The sandbanks rose up in places to almost twenty-five metres, reflected in the pale emerald of the river. It was unsettlingly vivid.

I wasn't paddling hard, but the four people ahead of me weren't paddling at all. They were drifting—eating and drinking and talking. I'm not brilliantly equipped for casual conversation with strangers at the best of times and I resented their presence. I started paddling hard, leaning forward and pulling with a full blade, going past them quickly, calling out hello. I wanted the river to myself. When I'd put enough distance between us, I let up and set my paddle across the gunwales and caught my breath. The thought that David had moved beneath me six months earlier, nudged along by the current, wouldn't leave.

The distinct green of the river reminded me of Lake O'Hara in the Rocky Mountains, a beautiful, difficult-to-get-to resort where David had once worked. The green of the lake was the result of light reflecting off deposits of marl—a mixture of clay and calcium carbonate.

Those were among David's happiest days. He'd been working at Lake O'Hara Lodge when the actor Peter O'Toole arrived to stay, alone and frail-seeming. He was hiding out after fleeing the set of *Caligula,* a movie being produced by *Penthouse* magazine's Bob Guccione and shot in Italy. The original script had been written by Gore Vidal, though he disowned the film after Guccione inserted graphic sex scenes with Penthouse pets into the final cut. O'Toole played Tiberius to Malcolm McDowell's Caligula.

David described O'Toole as surprisingly shy. There was a tradition of guests and staff having a talent night at the end of their stay. David had knocked on O'Toole's door and asked him to participate.

"I can't imagine what I would do," O'Toole said.

"You could read something, if you like," David said. "A poem."

O'Toole agreed, and so he stood in front of the assembled guests and read a poem. David noticed that his hands were shaking and thought it odd that one of Britain's greatest actors would be nervous reading in front of a small crowd in the middle of nowhere. Afterwards, David asked him about it and O'Toole said he'd always had stage fright. And he was no longer drinking (though smoking a fair amount of pot, apparently), which didn't help.

Since David had gone missing, I had read a pile of books on suicide. One of them was *Autopsy of a Suicidal Mind* by Edwin Shneidman, which I had taken out of the library based solely on the title. The book examined a single, lengthy suicide note written by a thirty-three-year-old physician to whom Shneidman had given the pseudonym of Arthur. The note and the details of Arthur's life were presented to various psychiatrists, who weighed in on Arthur's plight. "This is a case of a young man searching for authenticity, identity and individuation," one of them said. Aren't we all.

Reading the book, I was struck by how many superficial similarities there were between Arthur and my brother. Like David, Arthur had severe issues with food; he would only eat meat with no sauce on it and wouldn't eat fruit or vegetables. Like David, he sucked his thumb until he was six. As a child, David ate roast beef with butter on it, mashed potatoes, spaghetti without sauce, chicken noodle soup and not much else. He sucked his thumb so aggressively and persistently that the skin was chafed and bleeding. When the doctor prescribed a medication to put on my brother's thumb to prevent him sucking it, some distasteful pink ointment, David licked it off like it was ice cream.

Arthur had a brother who was two years older and more athletic and academically inclined, a parallel to our situation. Arthur was witty and brilliant at hiding his depression and compartmentalizing his life, as David was.

And both Arthur and David killed themselves at a point when things were going well. It seems a paradox—to endure such pain, and then when life gets better, to end it. For some people the pain is so incapacitating they aren't able to organize their own death. They don't have the initiative or the will. But as they begin to feel better, they are suddenly capable of killing themselves, and some of them do. They seem happier to others, because the end is in sight. That new sunniness, which friends and family interpret as an end to a long, difficult depression, is actually resolution.

Each of these men, Arthur and my brother, had attempted suicide once before. For some, one attempt is enough. The consequences are suddenly clear, like in a childhood game that goes off the rails where someone is injured. But for others, the unsuccessful attempt is the first critical step. It demonstrates they have it in them. With that first attempt, which my family and I didn't know about, my brother had statistically moved one step closer.

Arthur's attempt had been when he was fifteen. He'd gone away for a camp weekend and spent time socializing with popular kids, something he'd been excluded from. He'd had contact with a nice girl. He was filled with joy, which was immediately displaced by the fear that his life could follow this pattern: long stretches of isolation and depression interspersed with a few moments of tentative pleasure. He tried to kill himself by taking an overdose of Tylenol.

Arthur's brother felt that if they'd known more they could have done something, they could have saved him. But his sister said his suicide was inevitable; there was nothing that anyone could have done.

I think David could have been saved. If only he'd reached out, as they say. Though perhaps he did, subtly. We rarely called each other, but he'd called me once, a few years earlier. Things weren't going brilliantly for him. I could tell he'd been drinking as he rambled through recent events— troublesome gigs, romantic problems, money issues. I suggested that maybe it was time to move back to Calgary. It had a bigger music scene, old friends, more job opportunities, a new start. "Yeah," he said, "yeah, maybe." I asked him about the northern darkness. It would have felt like a shroud to me. "I'm a night person," he said. We talked for a while. It was one of the few times in adulthood that I'd felt like an older brother.

Along with his depression, Arthur had debt and had suffered a romantic loss (some of his note is addressed directly to a girlfriend he had just broken up with), just like David.

As I read, I was aware that I was looking for patterns the way a lot of suicide researchers tend to. They'd found patterns that ran through countries (Lithuania, Kazakhstan, Slovenia and Japan all have high rates), and professions (dentists, doctors) and into marital status (divorced and single are more likely) to behaviours (heavy drinkers, heavy smokers, addicts). One study linked losing sports teams to suicide (for example, when the Montreal Canadiens are eliminated early from the playoffs, suicide rates go up in Quebec; when the Ohio Buckeyes football team wins, rates go down in Ohio). With teams that have become synonymous with loss, like the Chicago Cubs (until they won the World Series in 2016, they hadn't won since 1908), you would expect a rash of suicides every year. But there isn't. The reason, sociologists say, is that perpetual loss brings Cubs fans together.

There are a lot of theories but few hard truths when it comes to suicide. French psychologist Gustave Le Bon wrote, "Many men can easily do without truth, but none is strong enough to do without illusion." In one of its guises, suicide is the abandoning of all illusion: that we will become fitter and happier, that we'll get out of debt, find love, wake up to find that darkness has lifted and the sun is shining.

The patches of blue sky were gone, replaced by gun-metal cloud that somehow flattened the landscape, giving it a two-dimensional quality. The wind had picked up. At this point, my sleep deprivation was edging toward hallucination. I paddled past a large group of ravens on the south bank of the river, and Hitchcock's *The Birds* replayed disturbingly in my head, Tippi Hedren fighting off the crows and gulls. David had once been attacked by a crow; it landed on his head and pecked him and he was suitably traumatized.

I was looking for a sunken plane that I'd read about in a brochure. Somewhere in the river there were the remains of an Avro Anson plane, eerily visible through the clear water. A British training plane, it was stolen in 1964 and the man who stole it crashed into the river, killing himself. I floated past the foundations of a pump house that was built by the American military when they constructed the Alaska Highway during World War II. Another boon to the town. But I didn't see the plane.

The river suddenly and dramatically narrowed as I entered a gorge, defined by dark basalt rock that hadn't budged in millennia. The water was dotted with small whirlpools that made the canoe skittish, and the current picked up. The black volcanic tunnel was otherworldly. It didn't look real. It began to rain, softly at first. The sky behind me was completely black and the water had gone dark, reflecting the black walls. The rain began to hammer down. My only rain gear was a light nylon windbreaker, which didn't really help. I'd forgotten how miserable it can be paddling in the rain. On my voyageur trip, we'd found ourselves in the middle of a lake during a thunderstorm, a dangerous situation. The wind was strong, and we debated whether to keep paddling into it or retreat to the nearest shore, which was not in the direction our trip was heading. We kept going into the wind, heads down, pummelled by the wind, the rain so loud we had to yell to be heard inside the canoe. We were soaked and heavy and tired and paddled as hard as we could, waiting for lightning to hit us. When we got to shore, we rigged tarps and sat under them, wet and freezing. There was nothing to do but wait and nothing to do while waiting.

I came out of the gorge into Schwatka Lake and paddled hard through the rain. I was exhausted. It wasn't the burning exhaustion of a sprint gone on too long, but a fatigue that consumed my limbs and my brain. I was sick of paddling. The bush pilot's shack was supposed to be somewhere here, but it was raining so hard I had trouble seeing the shore clearly, everything a grey green. At last I spotted a shack with a seaplane beside it in the lee of a small outcropping—it must be the one. I paddled to shore and pulled the canoe up and knocked on the door.

The pilot answered the door, then picked up the phone and called the outfitter. While we waited for the outfitter to arrive, the pilot told me they had pulled a body out of the water three nights earlier.

I asked who'd found him. Found David.

"A diver for the hydro company. His job is to inspect the dam, go down and inspect the gates, take out anything that's going to be a problem. He was with his son. They'd come in by plane, landed on the river. The son's a marathon runner. Kid runs into town to get their truck and on the way he sees someone in the water. Apparently, they'd been told to keep an eye out. The body was close to the bank, covered with silt and sand. Must have spent the winter down there. Police came and took him out with a grappling hook."

I asked if he wouldn't mind showing me where the body was found. I didn't tell him that the body was my brother's. He walked out of the shack and pointed to an eddy farther along the shore. "There, right where you see those rocks." I walked along the shore and stared uselessly at the spot for a time, then went back to the shack. "He was a local artist," the pilot told me. "He had the intention of killing himself."

The outfitter arrived and we loaded the canoe onto his trailer, and he drove me to the Marsh Lake Bridge to retrieve my car. When I got in, I turned the heat on. The rain was letting up, though the clouds lingered, a fact I was grateful for, a defence against the light.

———

Back in my room, I took a hot shower and put on clean clothes and went for a walk, past The 98, one of the places David had frequented—a one-storey building with a facade that made it look like a set for a western. It had four dirty windows, each blocked with a different material. Outside, a man was smoking a cigarette, his shirt open to reveal a canvas of angry ink. His nose was a curved beak with a bandage across it and his mouth a thin line, giving him the look of a bird of prey. He stared at me, apparently affronted by my presence.

I went to a restaurant, ordered a pizza and drank two glasses of wine, then a third, telling myself it would help me sleep. I lingered in the benign glow, examining my fellow diners. There was a table of German men, hearty and square and red-faced. I'd been told the Germans are big on hunting moose. A man I knew used to guide them, reciting Robert Service poems by the fire at night, assuring them that the moose they'd bagged was large, legendary. I finally left, thinking I might go for a last walk around the town. So much of David's life had been lived in these few blocks. I realized I couldn't bear another tour and went back to my hotel, dreading another sleepless night. I made notes, watched part of a black and white film, drank another glass of wine. I slept fitfully and endured a series of Dali-esque dreams. When I woke up at 4 a.m., it was with the sense that I would never sleep again, that I no longer needed it. I would be lucid and wide-eyed and have the focus of a peregrine falcon for the rest of my days.

My flight was at seven. I packed and paid the bill and drove to the airport and returned the car. I was suddenly seized with regret at not having gone to look at David's body. Over the last decade of his life, I had seen him for perhaps a week, and in the end I had taken the coroner's advice and looked away. I should have faced him. His pain must have been etched on his battered face. There would have been the visceral proof. And now I imagined him, the boy of my memory obliterated by the damaged man.

I walked out to the tarmac and boarded the plane. The unyielding sun came through my window. The plane rose and banked to the southwest, the city laid out like a board game, then quickly behind me.

7

AFTERMATH

We held a memorial service for David at my parents' spacious condo in Calgary. Old bandmates reunited and played a few songs. One of them told me that, musically, David had made them who they were. My family took some of his ashes up to Lake O'Hara in the Rocky Mountains, where we knew he'd been happy. We climbed a steep path overlooking the beautiful emerald-coloured lake, and each of us took a pinch of ash and scattered it to the wind, his daughter, Ivy, first. We laid more of his ashes in Jumping Pound Creek below our old house in the country, near where David had been married for the first time. My mother, who cries at everything—parades, sappy commercials, Robbie Burns poems—wept hard, her grief still raw. I said my final goodbyes to David and laid him to rest.

———

This turned out not to be true. One of the problems with suicide is it continues to raise questions, most of them a version of Why did they do it? The journey I'd started six months earlier—reading books and articles on suicide, interviewing people—intensified rather than diminished. When people die from suicide, one of the things they leave behind is suicide itself. It becomes a country. At first I was a visitor, but eventually I became something like a citizen.

I'd requested a copy of David's autopsy report, and it arrived a few weeks later in the mail. The medical cause of death was stated as "diphenhydramine Intoxication and Drowning." Diphenhydramine is the active ingredient in Nytol, the sleep medication. His liver showed trace elements of ethyl alcohol as well as benzoylecgonine, the primary metabolite of cocaine. He must have gone on a two-day farewell tour.

I had initially wondered if he had received some dire health news and was just foreshortening the inevitable. His lifestyle was spectacularly unhealthy, and he coughed like a retired coal miner. Perhaps lung cancer, those decades of smoke—both pot and cigarette—wafting through his body, finally presenting a bill. After being slim all his life, he had put on some weight in his forties. His heart, his liver, his lungs; there were several candidates for ruin.

With his vegetable-free diet he could have been suffering from scurvy, for all I knew. But the autopsy showed he was in serviceable health, at least.

I interviewed a few psychiatrists who dealt with suicide, read more articles, went to government websites, made loose plans to go to suicide conferences in exotic locations, drifted around the suicide world like a wraith.

The family quietly contracted around David's absence. I called my parents more often, went out to see them when I could. On one trip to Calgary, my father and I biked along the path that runs along the Bow River. In his eighties, he still went to the university gym three times a week and cycled regularly. We pedalled along the north bank toward the zoo, then crossed over and came back along the south bank and stopped and sat on a bench for a bit, staring at the river.

"This is where I sit and look at the river and think about David," he said. It was one of the few things he'd ever said about his son's suicide. I was suddenly aware of how much David's death had taken out of him. Such an obvious fact, but my sense of it had been muted until this moment.

My mother was more outwardly emotional. How had her son slipped away? When we spoke of him, though, it was always happily, recalling childhood anecdotes.

My parents eventually sold the lovely old nineteenth-century Steinway piano (may have been played by Franz Liszt, the ad read, though the pertinent fact was that it had been played by David), and I was surprised at how affected I was by its absence. My mother didn't play; my father, rarely. Perhaps they couldn't bear to have it there, reminding them of David; the closest thing to a grave—uplifting to visit once in a while but impossible to live with. I would have loved to have had it, though it would have cost a fortune to restore and to ship to Toronto and I didn't have anywhere to put it. And, of course, I couldn't play the bloody thing. Still, I felt bereft.

While suicide remains mysterious, in large part because the person is gone, survivors of loss have been studied in detail. There is consensus that mourning suicide is more complicated than mourning other deaths. It can be accompanied by shock, denial, guilt, sadness and anger. And often by the need to understand why. "This need to understand 'why' may be a difficult path," a mental health site warned, "as the circumstances surrounding the loved one's death could be unclear or not easily known. Some questions may never be answered."

Stages of grief were laid out: acute, integrated (gradually getting back to some kind of normalcy) and complicated. The clinical definition of "complicated" is an inability to reintegrate into normal life. Grief for a suicide is complicated primarily by guilt and by the incomprehension that we carry. For a long time, I didn't know what to say to anyone about David's death.

The first person I knew who killed himself came from a neighbouring family that seemed Kennedy-esque in its gifts—with an embarrassment of beauty, money, intelligence and athletic prowess. One of the family's four sons had died after intentionally (it was thought) driving a jet boat into a cement bridge support on the Red River. Not long after, another brother took his life. Along with my grief was bafflement. They had, as the cliché goes, everything to live for. It reminded me of the Simon and Garfunkel song, "Richard Cory," where the man with everything goes home and puts a bullet in his head. For more than a decade, these two brothers were the only suicides of people I knew.

The next was a journalist friend. We'd met at a literary event in Montreal, where we were both living in the eighties, and he approached and introduced himself as Stephen. He was the arts reporter for the national newspaper. I was a writer, he was a writer—we should know each other, he said. He had the good manners of his class, his brother a member of Parliament, his father a senator. Private school and summers in cottage country; a gracious upper-crust life that now has a remains-of-the-day quality. He invited me to a play that he was going to review in the east end of town. It was a German theatre group, he said, highly acclaimed.

The theatre was entirely black. Above the stage was a complicated-looking steel mechanism. After a few minutes of nothing happening, the mechanism began to shimmy a bit. Something was drifting down. It turned out to be flour; the mechanism was a giant flour sifter. The fine powder drifted down onto the black stage. Some of it drifted into the front rows, and there was coughing. After enough flour was on the stage, a man dressed in black came out and moved in a skating motion in his stocking feet. In the white powder, black lines appeared where he dragged his feet. He drew the simple outline of a fish: an ellipse with a triangular tail attached. Harsh mechanical music played. Half an hour later, he'd created the outline of, I think, a cat.

Stephen leaned over and whispered, "I owe you."

An hour later, there were a few more stick drawings made by Germans wearing black. The flour was everywhere. A lot more coughing.

Stephen leaned over again. "I'll do your taxes," he said.

He and I used to play tennis at the public courts in the eastern shadow of Mount Royal. He had grown up with tennis lessons and understood the game implicitly, though he wasn't a natural athlete. I had come to tennis late and was self-taught but more athletic. We were a good match. He was patient and limited. I attacked relentlessly and unsuccessfully, trying to kill the ball. "You have the tennis game of a low-percentage serial killer," he once told me. We'd play tennis, then go for a lazy Sunday brunch in the neighbourhood and talk about the mysteries of Montreal.

A year later he moved back to Toronto. In a few years I moved back as well. I saw him at parties, a tall, languid man with a drink and a story. Then I read in the morning paper that he was dead. A mutual friend told me he'd disappeared for a few days, wasn't in touch with his wife or family or friends. He had suffered from depression on occasion (I hadn't known) and they were worried. They called the police. Oddly, he surfaced to conduct an interview he had scheduled, professional to the end, but didn't get in touch with anyone else.

It was February and bitterly cold. He went into a ravine, one of those ribbons of parkland and homelessness that snake through the city. Under a busy overpass, he lay down and cut his wrists. Because it was so cold, he died of hypothermia rather than blood loss. He was discovered by a homeless man who alerted passersby, who called the police.

I went to his funeral, a grand, sombre affair. The city's elite overflowed the Anglican church nave and into other church spaces. The eulogist, a mutual friend, began, "Well, he wasn't much of a squash player . . ."

His death was a surprise to me. Friends who knew him much better than I deconstructed him in memoriam in the hope of making some sense of it. He'd been born into wealth, was a talented writer, and his wife was pregnant at the time. No one could explain why he would have done it.

Before my brother took his life, these were the only suicides I'd been personally affected by. But after his death, I felt like I was weathering a deluge of suicides. Partly this was because people would tell me of suicides in their own families, as if to console me. But I also found myself drawn to the obituary pages, seeking them out. Those who read the obits (and we are legion) know there are essentially three modern ways to die: suddenly, peacefully, and after a brave battle with cancer. "Suddenly" doesn't always mean suicide; it can be an accident or an unexpected heart attack. But the word is often used euphemistically for suicide. You can usually tell from the tone, the institution they suggest for donations in lieu of flowers. I always check to see how old they are. Many are middle-aged, men and women in their forties or fifties, and their deaths come as a surprise to loved ones.

A few years after David died, I got a call from a friend in Calgary.

"Rusty's dead," he said.

"What? What happened."

"He killed himself. Hung himself from his balcony."

The circumstances were vague. Rusty had lived in Mexico for years, had returned and embraced some kind of middle-aged renewal. He was getting in shape—walking ten thousand steps every day, measured with a pedometer. His Mexican world was murky and louche, but it was behind him. He was clean, back in God's country, though involved with a difficult woman. Then his sad, enigmatic death.

A year later, I was watching my eleven-year-old son play hockey in a gloomy, Soviet-inspired, suburban arena when the same friend phoned to say that another old friend had killed himself. Someone we'd known in university, a witty, elfin man who was doing something with computers on the coast. I hadn't seen him in twenty years.

I wondered what could have happened and called his widow. She told me that he'd never quite found a career. He had a master's degree and had done a wide range of things: worked in a bookstore, taught English as a second language, travelled the province trying to get ultimate Frisbee into the high-school sports curriculum. He'd been a technical writer, worked in advertising. Finally, he was involved in interactive technologies. He was intellectually restless, and as he got older, he was increasingly in conflict with co-workers and tended not to last long at jobs.

She said he'd gone to Europe for an interactive technology conference. He was there presenting an idea. It didn't go so well. "I picked him up at the airport—he was so exhausted and defeated," his wife said. "I'd never seen him like that." He was in his early fifties at this point.

Not long after that trip, he came downstairs and told his wife to take him to the hospital; he was worried that he might kill himself. He spent three days in the psychiatric ward. The doctor advised him to take time off work and prescribed antidepressants. He spent the summer in therapy and seemed to recover. He did some consulting, working out of their house.

He got a job with a company that did interactive displays. He was happy at first, but quickly became frustrated and angry. His co-workers were in their twenties and thirties, and he wasn't in charge—the traditional hierarchy was now inverted, with the young dictating to the old. He came home and drank wine and railed about the company, and quit after four months. On good days, he started drinking wine at dinnertime. On bad days he started at noon.

Their dog died, a blow, but they got another and it gave him a new lease on life. He had an idea for an app for dog owners to get together in the park for dog play dates. He talked to people in dog parks about it, then talked to people he knew in the industry. For a while he was buoyed by this possibility, then he suddenly decided it wouldn't work.

He unravelled very quickly after that, his wife said. He didn't want anyone to know how depressed he was because he didn't want to go back to the psychiatric hospital. He wasn't sleeping, was eating little and drinking a lot.

It was clear that he'd planned his death over the course of several weeks. He didn't want his wife to be alone when she found him, so he arranged for her sister to come for a visit. His original idea was to kill himself when his wife was picking up her sister at the airport. But she called from the airport to say the battery light was flashing in the car and maybe they should take it in. So he postponed his suicide until after he'd dealt with the battery.

The next day his sister-in-law hurt her knee, and he said it looked serious, that she needed to go to a clinic. She and his wife were gone a few hours. When the two women returned, his wife saw a note on the island in the kitchen. He often left notes, saying he'd gone out, when he'd be back. This one said that he'd decided to kill himself and to call 911. She screamed his name and he answered from upstairs. She ran up to find him covered in blood. He had cut himself, starting with his wrists, then moving to his throat, slashing desperately.

She called 911 and the ambulance came. Miraculously, he survived. He was in the hospital for a week. The first day he was there, a guard was stationed outside his door. But he convinced the doctors that he had made a mistake, that he wanted help, that he wanted to live. There wasn't any room in the psychiatric wing, and he was in a regular room. After the first night, there was no longer a guard at the door. After a week, he had healed enough to leave his room. He walked down the hallway into the visitor's lounge and onto the balcony, where he jumped. He hit the pavement and died, one day shy of his fifty-eighth birthday.

He left a five-page letter that was coherent, moving and

heartbreaking. He said he was unable to cope with the rapid change in the world, that he had failed in his profession, that he was a failure as a provider. He couldn't see a way out of his pain, couldn't face going through this over and over again.

I wondered at the kind of pain that produced such determination, that violence. He was a gentle soul. I recall him as a young man once answering the door naked, saying it was his Pondicherry leisure suit (referring to one of the hottest cities in India).

I wondered what would have happened if the European conference had gone brilliantly. Would a few altered moments in his life have changed the outcome? Many of us ponder these moments—*what if*? Each bad break another blow until finally we are unable to get up.

In middle age, I have known eight people who have killed themselves (all men) and three (two women, one man) who have attempted it. These figures are borne out by the statistics; people aged forty to fifty-nine now have the highest rate of suicide, more than youth and seniors combined, and men make up 80 percent of middle-aged suicides.

My generation's suicide rates are 60 percent higher than those of my father's generation. In our forties and fifties, a relative oasis of financial and family stability, we are increasingly in despair. My brother and these friends are part of a dismaying trend.

Historically the two most vulnerable times for suicide were adolescence and old age. In both groups, alienation can be a factor. Adolescence is confusion and doubt and finding a role for yourself. The elderly face some of the same issues: their utility vanishing, their health suspect, their thoughts unreliable. But between these two troubled poles, as a group, we have tended to be content. In mid-life, we are capable, if not assured, of love, work and family. We are between the financial yearning of our twenties and the looming destitution of our eighties. Delusional, perhaps, but happy nonetheless.

Mid-life used to be a lull in the suicide world, and statistics tended to be both low and stable. Until recently there weren't many academic studies of middle-aged suicide because there were so few of them. That has changed in the twenty-first century.

We approach the age of fifty from a variety of angles. There is the smugness of the well prepared, the triumphalism of the toned and youthful. But most of us approach warily. It is the first decade that really demands a reckoning—physical, financial, spiritual. It's hard not to look back on your life and judge.

In February 1964, my brother and I sat in front of our black and white TV set watching the Beatles debut on *The Ed Sullivan Show*. Was there ever a happier sound? In that one moment, millions of us were unconsciously pulled in the same direction: toward the seductive power of youth. And here were the simple, happy anthems. By the end of that decade our generation, like the Beatles, got more complicated and began to drift apart. Though we were always fragmented by class and gender and geography and politics, and, within the eighteen-year span (1946–1964) accorded the baby boomers, by age. We were a diverse group that became, in middle age, even more diverse. Set loose upon the world in exhilarating numbers, an entitled army born in the conflicting shadows of consumerism and idealism, we marched under many banners, but the most glaring was Youth. We felt we defined the word, we revelled in it, then hoarded it, refusing to give it up to the next generation. Leonard Cohen once said that in today's culture, you can hang on to the idea of youth until the age of sixty, but then you have to face the music.

8

LOST BOYS

One of the first studies done on the sudden spike in middle-aged suicide was published in 2010 by Rutgers sociologist Julie Phillips and three colleagues, titled "Understanding Recent Changes in Suicide Rates among the Middle-aged: Period or Cohort Effects?" Period effects are historical or cultural events that affect everyone, though they have a disproportionate effect on certain groups. The Great Crash of 1929, for example. But there wasn't anything particularly cataclysmic in the period Phillips examined, which was 1999 to 2005.

The other large-scale cause, from a sociological standpoint, is cohort effect. Because the boomers are the largest cohort of the twentieth century, there is greater competition for limited resources. In her study, Phillips found that the biggest increase in suicide was among those boomers who were unmarried and without a college degree. This supported the idea that competition for economic resources was taking a toll on those who were least qualified professionally, and without the economic and moral support of a partner.

Sociologists have also found relatively high rates of depression among boomers, although this could be due in part to greater awareness and more frequent diagnoses than in the more stoic generation that preceded us (often referred to by sociologists, for good reason, as the Silent Generation). And of course, there are high rates of substance abuse, an area where we are the generational champions.

Sociological studies of boomers aren't always flattering. We are seen as a group that hasn't developed the coping mechanisms that previous cohorts have. We are overly idealistic and haven't faced adversity. There is a sense of entitlement that came with our sheer numbers.

I called Phillips and asked about her research. She told me that baby boomers have always had high rates of suicide. In the seventies, the twenty- to twenty-four-year-old group had a rate that was triple that of our parents at that age. "Boomers may have a unique risk that they carry with them through the course of their lives," Phillips said. At every age, boomers' rates are far higher than those of any generation that came before, and they are also higher than those of subsequent generations. We are especially in despair in middle age.

"Clinical studies clearly show that knowing someone who committed suicide is a risk factor for later doing it yourself," Phillips said. "The high rate in adolescence could actually be contributing to the high rates in middle age among boomers, but at this point, we are just speculating."

Generations following in our annoying wake seem to be coping better. Phillips speculated that as new family and work structures become the norm, and the modest economic expectations for the millennials take root (not owning a house or car, having six different careers), suicide rates will go down. "People will recalibrate their expectations." And perhaps they have. The American Foundation for Suicide Prevention cites that in 2016 boomers had the highest rates of suicide (19.72 per 100,000), while the youngest group, aged fifteen to twenty-four, roughly corresponding to the millennials (born between 1982 and 2000), were significantly lower (13.15 per 100,000).

And what of old age? What will happen when boomers actually get old, when no amount of yoga or surgery or mindfulness exercises can disguise that fact?

"There is a good possibility the rates will be even higher still," Phillips said. "Usually as we age, we become more religious, but we haven't seen that with boomers. They aren't coming to Jesus."

Five years after Julie Phillips published her findings, things had gotten worse for the white boomers, in particular. "Something startling is happening to middle-aged white Americans. Unlike every other age group, unlike every other racial and ethnic group, unlike their counterparts in other rich countries, death rates in this group have been rising, not falling." This is the opening paragraph in a 2015 *New York Times* article that reported on the research of two Princeton economists, the husband-wife team of Angus Deaton and Anne Case. Deaton had just won the Nobel Prize for Economic Science. He and Case analyzed data from the Centers for Disease Control and Prevention, and concluded that middle-aged North American Caucasians were alone in their decline.

Deaton noted that it wasn't diabetes or heart disease that had caused this spike, it was suicide, substance abuse, liver disease and overdoses of heroin and prescription opioids. "Only H.I.V./AIDS in contemporary times has done anything like this," he wrote.

Most of the casualties (seven out of ten) were white men.

Newspapers picked up the story ("Toxic Masculinity May Be Quadrupling the Suicide Rate for Canadian Men," "Baby Boomer Suicide Rate Rising, May Go Higher with Age"). The word "epidemic" was thrown around. The Centre for Suicide Prevention published a toolkit for middle-aged men titled "Men & Suicide: A High-Risk Population," which included warning signs and risk factors.

Men's suicide rates are more than three times those of women (27.1 per 100,000 versus 8.1 per 100,000), though women make more attempts. This discrepancy is partly the result of men using more lethal methods—guns rather than sleeping pills, for example. The sociological literature cites several reasons for high rates in men. One is economic. An aging workforce cannot retrain with the speed of change in the economy. Jobs are exported, made redundant, given to younger workers. Industries vanish. Another is the increasingly blurry definition of what it is to be male.

This has been going on for decades, and has prompted periodic calls for either a new version of masculinity, or reverting to an old version. In 1990, *Iron John* arrived, a mythopoetic treatise that had us reverting to hairy mammals howling around a campfire. More recently, there are the blunt, unpoetic goals of the Proud Boys, a "fraternal organization of Western Chauvinists" that wants to recreate a

1950s world. Among their slogans is "Venerate the house-wife." Two of the four initiation rituals involve fighting (one calls for fighting other Proud Boys; another for beating up left-wing protesters). There are other movements, some nostalgic for a time when patriarchy was clear and dominant, others simply trying to find an acceptable definition of masculinity.

My childhood was composed of masculine rituals, many of them arcane, involving sports, bicycles, wrestling matches, slingshots, lighter fluid and BB guns. A friend and I put on football helmets and sunglasses and shot at each other with our BB guns in his basement. There were bicycle races and games of chicken. We jumped out of trees or off roofs, fought one another. Who had the courage to ring the door-bell of the suspected witch's house? Who had the nerve to race out of the woods onto the putting green, scoop up a just-landed chip shot and tear back into the woods with the ball, chased by a lumbering, bleating golfer.

The comic books of my childhood carried ads for Charles Atlas exercise equipment, a series of panels titled "The INSULT that made a man out of Mac." Mac was a skinny guy at the beach who gets sand kicked in his face by a bully, at which his beautiful girlfriend immediately drops him. He builds muscles, returns to the beach (in the space of two comic-strip panels) and punches the bully in the face. His former girlfriend melts in his arms, cooing, "Oh Mac! You ARE a real man after all."

I was a skinny guy and I sent away for a set of Weider weights, which were delivered by mail, all hundred-plus pounds of them. They came with large photographic instruction sheets that had bodybuilder Dave Draper demonstrating bicep curls and squats. I worked out in my basement and posed in the mirror, waiting for the miraculous transformation.

A lot of masculine rituals were driven by hormones and stupidity. One afternoon my brother and I and a cousin who was visiting from the east lit firecrackers to see who could hold one the longest before tossing it away. Inevitably, this led to holding the firecracker until it went off, leaving our hands numbed by the percussive shock, the gunpowder residue a badge of honour.

That evening the community had a fireworks display for the May 24 weekend. Various dads milled around the box of elaborate fireworks they'd bought, more than half of them smoking. Inevitably, a cigarette landed in the box and ignited the fireworks and we got an impressive, if haphazard, display. The evening's entertainment was over in less than a minute, leaving the smell of gunpowder in the air. We filed home, briefly thrilled but ultimately disappointed. The infallible-seeming dads, an army of providers, had let us down.

I had a stern, cleft-chinned hockey coach who called us by feminine derivatives of our names (Donna, Josephine) when we lost, which was most of the time. I remember men on our block gathering around the open hood of a new car to marvel at the engine and talk about the carburetor. From the muddy perspective of childhood, they all seemed so capable. Some were, but others assumed different dimensions as I grew up. A man a few doors down suffered a "nervous breakdown." There were hapless fathers, an alcoholic, affairs, divorce. A friend's father, a silent, defeated man, broke a broomstick over his son's head. All these men of the Silent Generation had found themselves in the wrong life.

My father was a shining exception, a man who could do anything, it seemed, someone who always did the right thing. As an adolescent, I'd been beaten up by the father of a girl I knew who thought I'd been raiding his garden (I hadn't, though I was allied with the raiders). When I got home with my shirt torn, my lip bleeding (the weight training having been less effective than I'd hoped), my dad asked what had happened. The next morning we went over to the man's house. We found him sitting in his living room in a singlet, drinking beer, a tough guy who'd made it big doing something up north. He had a Cadillac and a swimming pool. His daughter was present, looking mortified. My father told the man that if he wanted to pick on someone, he should pick on him. After a tense moment—a version of the schoolyard, only with adults—the man took a sip of his beer, grunted something vaguely conciliatory, and we left.

In his book *Prime Green: Remembering the Sixties,* Robert Stone wrote of his own, slightly older generation in that time. Stone was born in 1937, safely among the Silent Generation. He was thirty years old in the Summer of Love, though he jumped into the counterculture with both feet, a rider on Ken Kesey's famous psychedelic bus, a bearded, acid-dropping explorer. "Our expectations were too high," he wrote of that time, "our demands excessive; things were harder than we expected. . . . We wanted it all; sometimes we confused self-destructiveness with virtue and talent, obliteration with ecstasy, heedlessness with courage. . . . We wanted to die well every single day, to be a cool guy and a good-looking corpse. How absurd, because nothing is free, and we had to learn that at last. Every generation must."

Boomers tore down traditional structures, or at least weakened them—divorce rates went up, church going went down, and trust in politicians eroded. Corporations were suddenly the enemy, and the appeal of spending your life working for a company, the way many of our parents had, withered. What replaced these traditional structures, ultimately, was the triumph of the individual. This was good in many ways, but in difficult times, it meant there was less to fall back on.

The social bonds that once held us together quietly faded. We move around more; we are dispersed geographically. Nationalism is in decline. It has always been in decline in Canada, that is its natural state. Even in the United States, that beacon of love-it-or-leave-it patriotism, it is faltering. Cries for unity during the 2016 US election were campaign fables, and the result left the country more divided than ever, caught in a vicious tribalism that shows no sign of waning.

Perhaps my generation wasn't designed for middle age, just as the previous generation wasn't designed for youth. When I look through my parents' photographs, I see alarmingly adult-looking twenty-five-year-olds. My parents were married when my mother was twenty-three, my father twenty-four.

They had a mortgage and two kids by the time my dad was twenty-seven. At that age, I was wandering a landscape of odd jobs and vague dreams, living in a cinderblock apartment, longing for unsuitable women. When my parents' generation reached middle age, they were solid citizens—mortgages, sedans, brogues and those Fred MacMurray haircuts. Most of them didn't experience youth the way we did. And certainly not for the same duration (fifty years, in some cases). My parents' generation seemed to inhabit middle age easily because they spent their whole lives there. Youth was a brief flash in first-year university before dating your future wife. Middle age went on forever.

We lived in the moment, as they say. This is good as long as the moment is good, if the moment holds promise and fellowship and a sense of possibility. But if the moment drags on, if it feels more like an Andy Warhol movie, a static shot of quotidian events that is going absolutely nowhere, then it isn't so good. David lived in the moment. He played late, slept late, had fun. He did what he loved until he no longer loved it.

I don't know if he suffered from depression, which is cited as a factor in 50 percent of suicides. He was never diagnosed, wasn't on any medication (other than self-medication). None of his friends described him as depressed. But like some of the other men I knew who killed themselves, he could no longer find a place for himself. He was part of a tidal wave of middle-aged male despair.

For many boomers, that generational identity that is so highly touted and lives gloriously in the nostalgic mist has frayed. The revolutionary fervour of the sixties still exists, though without revolutionaries now. What is left is the mythology.

Mythology is supposed to be a comfort; that is its point. But it no longer unites us. What unites us now? Age and debt, among other things. I didn't notice when debt became the central focus of so many lives around me, when conversations began to gravitate to housing prices and the high cost of daycare, or sports equipment, dance lessons or college tuition, depending on where you were on the continuum. When I was young, debt was an abstraction, and to some degree, it has remained one. And this, of course, is part of the problem.

My Scottish grandmother, Georgina Mainland, grew up in the Depression, and debt was as palpable to her as death. It was solid and tangible and destructive. Her husband, Donald, worked sporadically and was on a modest disability pension from a World War I injury. My grandparents never had a mortgage; my grandfather was a bricklayer by trade, and when they had saved enough money, they bought land and the materials to build a house. Don built it himself, and when it was finished, they made sure it stayed mortgage free.

My grandmother saved string and elastics, and mixed the remains of old paint cans together into an indeterminate beige-like colour that she used to paint the interior walls. She bought inexpensive cuts of meat that she roasted into asphalt, clipped coupons, and entered every contest in the world, once winning a complete Blue Bomber football uniform that she gave to me. She had a backyard vegetable garden and took in boarders and shunned restaurants (though this was partly her distrust of foreign cooks and their tricky spices and liberal views on hygiene). She bought everything on sale.

My parents were neither frugal nor spendthrift. They splurged occasionally (like the family trip to Europe). They had far more options than my grandparents had. My parents were young and optimistic, at a time when the world largely shared that youth and optimism.

My own generation was born into that optimism; it was a birthright. Debt is a form of optimism; the view that housing prices will rise and our equity will flourish, that stock portfolios will recover, that the job market will once more be lucrative and comprehensible. So borrowing isn't really a problem. At any rate, it's a necessity; debt is the only way most people can afford a house and a car. And it has come to live with us permanently, like an unfortunate relative whose table manners are suspect, whose opinions we don't share, who never lifts a finger: a drain on our lives. The ratio of household debt to annual income in 1965 was 60 percent; in 2017, it was 171 percent.

If debt is a product of optimism (and entitlement), it is also its enemy, and our optimism is vanishing now, it seems. A survey from the Pew Research Center noted that boomers' assessment of their quality of life is lower than that of both the preceding and succeeding generations. We are a gloomy group. It was a surprise to find that we've been gloomy for a while: the data suggests that this was the case twenty years ago, when late boomers were still in their twenties. And it isn't just our own economic situation that we're pessimistic about, but everyone's. We fear for our parents and our children, but mostly, of course, we fear for ourselves.

Three decades of data from the General Social Survey, a sociological survey created by the University of Chicago, note that boomers report that they have experienced less happiness than both younger and older people do. How can this be, given that the pursuit of self-fulfillment was central to so many of our lives? Happiness is a broad, unscientific concept. One of the things it is measured against is expectation.

We wanted so much. So much change, so much sex, so much love. And now money. The fact that the oldest boomers (born 1946–1955) have the highest levels of poverty since the generation born before World War I is a surprise. But that early generation grew up amid the long shadow of the Great War; their expectations were probably quite low. Coming out of the ample, stylish (in retrospect, anyway) bosom of the 1950s, boomers expected everything. We'll never be richer or younger than we are right now. And it isn't enough.

Growing older is an education in loss, a friend said, after two close friends died (a heart attack and a car accident) within months of one another. It isn't just friends and parents we lose as we grow older. We lose those parts of ourselves that were never fully realized—the unfulfilled potential.

I am always astonished by people who say, "If I had it to do over again, I wouldn't change a thing." I would. I'd change all kinds of things. I'd have stuck with the piano, not bought Nortel when it dropped to twenty dollars, forgone the odd regretted tryst and the crushed velour bell bottoms. I would have started writing earlier, I would have worked harder in school, I wouldn't have bought that International Travelall (an oversized station wagon that only farmers drove and got four miles to the gallon). I would have been more ambitious, more focused, more compassionate. I would have recognized earlier how important relationships are. In my twenties and thirties they came easily, but some have slipped away almost as easily for reasons I can't recall.

The suicide rate among baby boomers speaks of something collective and despairing. Don DeLillo wrote that history is longing on a large scale. It appears that my generation is longing for something, perhaps something obvious like love or community, or perhaps something we can't quite define, something that we sense as we muddle through middle age but that is just out of reach.

9

THE GHOST
IN THE MACHINE

I had lunch with a woman I'd known for decades. She asked what I was working on.

"A book on suicide."

"Have you ever considered it yourself?" she asked. Committing suicide, she meant.

"No." It was the truth. "Have you?"

"I think about it every day. It's not something I intend to do, but it's always there, an option."

She told me that most days she took the idea out and examined it, like a sharp sword passed down through generations of a military family, lethal and comforting.

"You don't need to worry," she added.

But I did. The worry stayed with me and I sometimes imagined her day, getting up in the morning and choosing life as if it was an outfit to wear. How for her death had become a daily companion. Each day they acknowledge one another, like an old married couple who no longer have much to say but still find comfort in each other's presence.

Death is everyone's companion, of course. It informs every life. But it was a shock to find out how many of us actually carry the idea of suicide around like a wallet. The National Survey on Drug Use and Health estimated that in the United States in 2008, 8.3 million adults had suicidal thoughts. Of those, 2.3 million made a suicide plan and 1.1 million made an actual attempt, with 666,000 ending up in hospital emergency rooms. Just over 36,000 succeeded.

The survey was the first scientific inquiry into suicidal ideation. Like so many suicide statistics, they induce doubt: Who can see into our dark thoughts? Still, Nietzsche may have been right when he wrote that the idea of suicide is a comfort for many.

Occasionally I find myself looking at people and wondering if they are carrying the idea of their own death around like a concealed weapon. The middle-aged woman at the Motor Vehicles wicket where I am renewing my driver's licence is wearing a knock-off Burberry scarf against the air-conditioning, assessing the lengthy line-up, her face pretty but worn, institutional weariness emanating from her like perfume. Perhaps she had her heart broken and then went on a series of online dates that further shook her faith in love and the future. After she processes our error-filled applications, dealing with the natural hostility we have for any government line-up, she'll take the overcrowded subway home to an empty condo and a screen filled with Netflix and drink a nice bottle of Bordeaux and take the pills she's been hoarding. Or perhaps tonight, just the Bordeaux.

Pete, a former bandmate of David's, sent me an email that read, "I've survived prostate cancer, and, most recently, have had surgery to remove skin cancer. Am I alright? I'm not sure. I sometimes lie awake at night and wonder whether or not Dave got it right. Does all of the worry, planning and work we do actually pay off? Is it worth the time and effort? Will I be happy at the end of the road? Perhaps these thoughts also crossed Dave's mind. While I am not suicidal, from the time I was in high school until the present, I have always considered suicide as an alternative to continuing to struggle with life. And maybe that's what Dave decided. The dark thoughts come very rarely and are easily subdued. But they do come and perhaps that is what Dave struggled with as well."

Many of us struggle with dark thoughts. And it's not always possible to tell who, and how dark. The children's author Robert Munsch (*Love You Forever, The Paper Bag Princess*) struggled with dark thoughts. He has written more than fifty children's books, almost all of them happy, loud celebrations of life. He has given exuberant, high-energy performances to appreciative audiences. Few people looked happier.

But several years ago, he publicly admitted to being bipolar and to using cocaine and being an alcoholic. This admission, as you might imagine, was revelatory. Since I had also written children's books, a magazine editor thought I would be the perfect person to write an article about Munsch.

I arranged for an interview and drove an hour or so west of Toronto to Guelph, where Munsch lived in a modest suburban house with his wife and children. He was doing a reading in Hamilton that day, an hour away, and the two of us drove there in his Honda Accord. He was sixty-five, still boyish, wearing a floppy white hat and sunglasses that made him look like a cross between a nine-year-old camper and Hunter S. Thompson. I heard traces of the manic energy of his books in his otherwise quiet, deliberate conversation, the uppercase emphasis of *Moira's Birthday* ("TWO HUNDRED PIZZAS! ARE YOU CRAZY?"). He told me that his grandfather had killed himself and that he had had long stretches where he was suicidal as well. "You can't trust your own thoughts," he said as he drove. "You think, 'Today would be a good day to kill myself.' TODAY WOULD *NOT* BE A GOOD DAY TO KILL MYSELF!!"

Munsch said he'd had few friends growing up and had few friends now; his life was eaten up by work and an extensive touring schedule. I asked him about his background. He grew up in Pittsburgh and worked outside Boston at a daycare in the seventies. His description of America at that time was dystopic—gutted inner cities, racially divided, Vietnam-addled. He was mugged in Boston and needed plastic surgery for his face. "It was like living in a war zone," he said.

He became depressed and began drinking to deal with it. The drinking spiralled and by 1986 he was attending Alcoholics Anonymous meetings. He went back and forth—sober, then drinking, quitting, then only drinking a glass of wine a week, then a glass of wine a day, then scotch in the morning, then back to AA.

He was fifty-nine, and one of the most successful children's authors in history (*Love You Forever* alone sold more than thirty million copies) when he turned to cocaine, at an age when most people are giving things up, certainly drugs.

"I'd drive to Toronto, to Sherbourne Street or Parliament, chat up people," he said. "I never had a secure connection. I gave money to a guy who said, 'Wait a minute, I'll be right back,' and disappeared." He occasionally did coke with whoever had sold it to him, all of them younger and poorer and more attuned to the street than he was. They sometimes thought he was a Clouseau-like undercover cop. It took him four years to quit, aided by the fact that he'd suffered a stroke. He told me all this as he drove. When we arrived in Hamilton and parked, he checked his cellphone to see how many sober/clean days he had. "I'm, let me see, here it is—235 days now. That's my clean date."

He was going to perform for a day camp at a school gymnasium. I looked around at the hundreds of kids, a wide age range that went from five to fourteen or so. A nightmare audience, really. Children can be restless and ruthless and unforgiving. At a school reading I once gave, two seven-year-old girls in the front row fought over a Barbie pen until one of them hissed "Fuck off, Madison" and yanked it away.

But Munsch won them all over. Even the cynical older kids, the ones who were probably already dabbling in online porn, whose innocence was long gone, who hadn't seen a picture book in years, went along with him. Munsch had once done as many as two hundred performances a year, but then the stroke left his memory diminished. There were hints of memory issues now, when he stalled for a moment, but the kids either didn't notice or forgave the lapses. He was beloved.

As we drove back to Guelph, Munsch ruminated on the show. "I do these shows and people like them," he said. "But afterwards, it's just me." The common lament of the performer, that they are most comfortable on a stage, most loved. And when they step offstage, they aren't entirely sure of who they are. Not long after our meeting, he gave up performing completely.

Which meant he'd effectively given up writing. He wrote his books onstage, telling stories to his audience, then rejecting ones that didn't work, honing the ones that did. Then he wrote it down. By any measure he'd had a brilliant career, but for decades he had lived with the fear of taking his own life.

The history of suicide is a history of that internal fear, the fear that today would be a good day to kill ourselves. In ancient Athens, suicides were buried outside the city, with the self-murdering hand cut off and interred separately, as if it were somehow responsible. In the Middle Ages in Europe, people who killed themselves were considered criminals and treated as such. People caught attempting suicide were hanged. The bodies of suicides were degraded, sometimes horrifically. In Britain they were hanged from a gibbet and left to rot. Or they were placed at a crossroads, a stake driven through the corpse, a stone covering their face to prevent the ghost from rising. In France, the corpses of people who killed themselves were dragged through the street and burned. Noblemen who committed suicide lost their rank and property—their woods cut, their land forfeited to the Crown.

The societal fear was that suicide was contagious, something that could be passed on like the plague. To some extent that is true, as evidenced by cluster suicides in schools, where one student kills himself and others quickly follow his example. Or in First Nations communities where suicide is the leading cause of death for those under the age of forty-four. In communities where there is collective despair, one person killing themselves can feel like permission for others who have been carrying the idea around.

Daniel Stern wrote in his novel *The Suicide Academy,* "Suicide is, in short, the one continuous, every-day, ever-present problem of living. It is a question of degree.

I'd seen them in all varying stages of development and despair. The failed lawyer, the cynical doctor, the depressed housewife, the angry teenager . . . all of mankind engaged in the massive conspiracy against their own lives that is their daily activity. The meaning of suicide, the true meaning, had yet to be defined, had yet to be created in the broad dimensions it deserved."

The meaning of suicide is elusive, which makes preventing it so difficult. It embodies so many factors—social (alienation), economic (unemployment), personal (depression, mental illness, alcoholism). It is a complex issue that hasn't found its poster child. The suicides that get a lot of attention are usually those of celebrities. Robin Williams's tragic end was discussed and analyzed for months. Kurt Cobain's suicide became iconic. Yet celebrity suicides don't inspire the same political or fundraising efforts as other celebrity problems or diseases. The Michael J. Fox Foundation has raised $450 million for research into Parkinson's disease, for example. By contrast, comedian Drew Carey, who attempted suicide when he was eighteen, offered a low-key, heartfelt public service announcement telling people to get help.

There remains a stigma with mental illness, fading, but still potent. And there is the problem of identifying who is at risk. With cancer and Parkinson's and multiple sclerosis, the victims are visible. With suicide, we don't always know.

Globally more than a million people take their own lives each year. Most years that is a toll greater than homicide and war. And there is a rough consensus among suicidologists that suicide is under-reported by as much as 60 percent. In 2013, reported suicides in the United States numbered more than deaths from car accidents, AIDS, or prostate cancer, and were almost on par with breast cancer. Yet suicide isn't widely studied or heavily funded. Suicide isn't a medical condition, it's an outcome. The worst outcome.

I've tried to inhabit the moment that my brother stepped into the river, to understand the weight he carried when he stood at the edge of the ice. Perhaps he was at a point where the psychic pain was like the sound of a waterfall, a roar that eclipsed all rational thought. No matter how meticulously planned, suicide is also an impulsive act. People spend months planning to jump, they condition themselves by walking to the bridge where they're going to jump. They climb onto the railing, then climb back down. They work up to it. But at that final second, they still have to jump, they have to make a decision.

What happens in that final second is now attracting attention from researchers. The Reasons to Go On Living Project, a research initiative at Hamilton's McMaster University, is studying that moment. A website allows those who have either attempted or seriously contemplated suicide to share their stories anonymously. They have jumped and survived, or miscalculated the sleeping pill dose and woken up, but they inhabited that moment. Their stories are posted online with the hope that others will read them and learn from those experiences. The site offers a graphic illustration of the adage that suicide is a long-term solution to a short-term problem.

The website states: "We are doing this . . . to understand how people's thinking changes after a suicide attempt. We do not understand the thinking processes that occur for people who choose to go on living after an attempt and there is very little research in this area. We believe that if we had a better understanding of how people found the strength to go living after an attempt, we might be able to better help people who are thinking of ending their lives, before they make an attempt."

The project was begun by Dr. Jennifer Brasch, who works in the Psychiatric Emergency Service at St. Joseph's Healthcare. I drove to Hamilton to talk to her. In a hospital waiting room before our interview, I assessed the patients who sat nearby. There was a woman in her thirties with amateurish tattoos who had a druggy fidget, like she was trying to escape her own skin. Another woman came in and sat beside her, followed by a third. They were all pretty tough looking, but these three strangers bonded with a speed I've rarely seen. Within minutes they were listing the anti-depressants they'd been on, which ones worked, other drugs that didn't do the trick, and a few that rocked their world.

"That one definitely didn't bring out the best in me," one of them said.

"No?"

"I put Mr. Clean in my husband's coffee."

"I'll bet that woke him up."

"Hahahaha."

After a few more anecdotes, the trio split up and I went in to see Brasch. I asked her where the idea for Reasons to Go On Living had come from. She told me that when people had attempted suicide but failed, and ended up in the emergency unit, she was called in to talk to them. "By the time I get to them they've usually been in the unit for at least a couple of hours," she said. "Fairly often people would look at me and say, 'What was I thinking? I couldn't do that. I didn't think about how much my wife cared, about my kids, about my job, about the cottage I'm building,' whatever it is. Something had happened between the suicide attempt and when I saw them. So we started asking patients, '*What* happened? What's different?' They had enormous difficulty articulating the shift that had taken place, from looking at death to choosing life. But something happened in there."

The stories that are posted on the Reasons to Go On Living website are, by turns, sad, uplifting, comforting and horrifying. A depressed woman whose son had been taken from her by social services decided to jump from a sixth-floor balcony. She wrote, "At the very last second as I hung onto the railing of the balcony I did not want to die but it was too late. I landed on the parking lot pavement." She suffered multiple, painful injuries.

A woman speeding toward an overpass support in her car, intent on killing herself, suddenly brakes and pulls over when she realizes she can't leave her children like that.

One woman wrote that she first attempted suicide when she was ten years old by swallowing a bottle of iodine. It didn't work. She grew up, got married, and was widowed young when her pilot husband was shot down during World War II. She remarried, had children, suffered postpartum depression and once more felt suicidal. She had shock treatments and thought about throwing herself off an overpass onto the busy highway below, but realized it would be terrible for the driver who hit her. During another bout of depression, she carried pills with her so she could take an overdose if the mood struck. She had six children and survived all her suicidal impulses, went to a recovery group and found yoga helpful. But the last paragraph of her entry is chilling.

"Now that I'm 85 years old, suicidal thoughts are constantly with me because I don't want to become a burden to my family. I have had a long and happy life, a wonderful family, a wonderful married life and feel very lucky that I did not succeed in committing suicide."

It was a "long and happy life," yet she wanted, on several occasions, to end it, and may yet do so. There are gaps in her logic, but suicide isn't logical. She contemplated it, tried it, then kept it at her side as an invisible friend.

When I asked Brasch what she expected to get out of the project, she replied, "Less than I'd originally thought when we started."

I could see why she would initially be so hopeful. Her

study addresses one of the biggest hurdles for suicide researchers: their subjects are all dead. But here are people who are alive, who have stepped back from the abyss. What did they see there? The answers are personal and idiosyncratic. Perhaps they have helped potential suicides to rethink their decision. Mostly what they illustrate is what it is to be human. One survivor offered this chilling quote: "You survive, but the call of the void never quite goes away. But you learn not to answer it."

David had guarded against the possibility of turning back at the last minute with alcohol and sleeping pills. At that point, he may not have been able to articulate a retreat, all language gone, his thoughts forming like a dark tidal pool stranded by the retreating ocean.

Harder science turned its gaze toward suicide. In 2011, John Mann, chief neuroscientist at the New York State Psychiatric Institute, conducted genetic tests on 412 people with depression, 154 of whom had attempted suicide. A variant of a gene called RGS2 appeared more often in the subjects who had tried to kill themselves, supporting the theory that there is genetic risk for suicide. Kurt Cobain had two uncles who killed themselves, Ernest Hemingway's father killed himself, as did two of his siblings and a granddaughter. If genetic testing can reveal suicidal tendencies, then precautions can be taken.

In 2017, researchers at Carnegie Mellon University in Pittsburgh took the scientific approach further. They developed a brain scan that can discern suicidal thoughts. Using a machine-learning algorithm and brain imaging, they examined thirty-four subjects, half with known suicidal tendencies, the other half without. All of them were given three lists of ten words each. The first list had death-related words (death, fatal), the second had positive words (praise, carefree), and the third had negative words (boredom, trouble). Magnetic resonance imaging (MRI) was done on them while they read the lists. The algorithm was applied to the resulting scans and distinguished the suicidal group 91 percent of the time.

This should be encouraging news. But when it comes to the human mind, science has often over-promised and under-delivered. Great hope has been invested in electro-convulsive therapy, in drugs as diverse as LSD and chlor-promazine for curing everything from depression to schizophrenia. While drugs and ECT have helped, they also caused a lot of damage along the way. The magic bullet approach often neglects social and human factors. Once we identify suicidal people, what do we do? If the predictive science pans out and is widely adopted, it will be both a help and a worry as parents identify a child as suicidal. They will do what many parents are doing now—whatever they can to help their child, while learning to live with that dark companion.

There is a woman I regularly see marching down Queen Street in Toronto muttering to herself. I wonder how she survives. She is bent over completely, her back at a ninety-degree angle to her legs. She is always dressed in black, perhaps the same clothes. I saw her once in an upscale shoe store, muttering, her head tilted up to see the world. No one approached her. A mix of fear and pity; what could we do for her? We avoided her as if she was dangerous. Don't make eye contact.

She was likely in her seventies and, despite her obvious and ongoing misery, she soldiered on. One foot in front of the other in what must have been a painful succession. Something primitive, something at the cellular level, told her to keep trudging.

At the cellular level, we all want to live. But cells make sacrifices—millions of cells kill themselves in aid of our survival. Cells kill themselves when they become a threat to the organism; cells infected by viruses fall on their swords. The cells that kill the virus have to go too. After they've killed the invader, lymphocytes die. They are brave and necessary, but now that the threat is gone, we don't want them around.

Even when our mind feels otherwise, the body perseveres in its struggle to survive. When a young woman with anorexia starves herself, exhausting her fat reserves, the body tries to protect itself by growing hair as insulation. At the biological level, we crave life.

Suicide is an argument with our own biology. The body states repeatedly, under awful conditions—grinding poverty, disease, disfigurement, abuse—that it wants to continue. The mind respectfully nods in agreement, then pulls the trigger.

10

DEAD POET SOCIETY

Several years after David's death, I woke up on a dull spring morning to see two emails. One was from the public library notifying me that the copy I'd ordered of *Why People Die by Suicide* had come in. The other was from an old friend, a poet named Murdoch who was living on the coast, telling me he was recovering from a suicide attempt. In the damp cold of January, he had stepped in front of an eighteen-wheeler. He survived being hit by a truck, sustaining a broken clavicle and other injuries. This was the first I'd heard of it. I hadn't seen him in more than a decade.

I had met Murdoch in grade twelve. I was a new kid who had moved to Calgary a few weeks after school started; he quit the day I arrived. He came into the diner across from the school where a lot of students ate lunch, and where I sat, unsuccessfully trying to fit in. He had long, blond hair and his face was furrowed in anger like one of the monsters from *Where the Wild Things Are*. He yelled to the assembled: "I'm quitting this fucking prison, and if any of you have half a brain, you'll quit too." He slammed the door and we went back to our lunches. I didn't actually meet him until months later, when a friend introduced us. "I'm a poet," Murdoch said defiantly, an exotic concept in that oil town.

On my way to school, I used to pass his family's house, which sat alone on a small acreage, waiting to be engulfed by the quickly expanding city. Our school was on the western outskirts of Calgary, and we were living in a large, charmless new house while my father was designing a place for us out in the country. Beyond our brand-new subdivision was empty prairie and a few corrals that still held horses. There were horses and cows and chickens outside Murdoch's place. Inside, in his own description, was a family of porridge-eating hillbillies, and the chaos that comes with eleven children. His father was a handsome, hard-drinking man who wore one pant leg inside his cowboy boot and the other outside, someone who could do a hundred things, from breaking horses to driving trucks to building houses.

During a savage winter where the temperature dipped to minus forty, the jerry-rigged addition to Murdoch's house fell away when the cinder block foundation cracked. The bedroom containing several children separated from the house, the father standing at the opening like Ahab on the foredeck, wondering why God was punishing him. He shored it up and patched it, and the family survived this calamity as it had survived others. Murdoch's father eventually went blind.

After university, I drifted into the local arts scene and there was Murdoch, a poet with a book of poems. An admirer of the Beat writers, he helped bring Allen Ginsberg and William Burroughs to town for readings. He was a gregarious man, steeped in the romantic notion that a poet needed to suffer for his art. He saw Dylan Thomas as a role model rather than a cautionary tale. He wore a series of dark, thrift-shop, narrow-lapelled suit jackets, and he was always doing something with a cigarette, lighting it, putting it out, waving it as he railed about local philistines or rock and roll losing its way. He was a true believer who embodied the best of those hopeful counterculture tropes: to love one another (despite an occasionally Irish temper), to be individuals in a sea of conformity, to stick it to the man. No one I knew bought into the sixties with more conviction than Murdoch did.

I certainly didn't. I loved the music and lived for the promise of sex in whatever guise—free love or its less elevated versions. But I was never in danger of being hip—a girl in twelfth grade once told me I looked like a substitute English teacher. Marijuana made my eyes red and induced a monumental lethargy. After smoking a joint, I didn't want to go anywhere or do much other than lie on someone's shag carpet and listen to *Tubular Bells* through headphones that weighed ten pounds. A woman once accused me of being "bourgeois," a term hurled as an insult. It was largely true.

But I loved books and wanted to write, and Murdoch did too, and we were joined by that. He believed in the transcendence of experience and quoted the William Blake line "The road of excess leads to the palace of wisdom." He wasn't the first to take it literally. He drank and chain-smoked and wrote poems and raged, and had a natural charm and was excellent company.

When friends formed a band, Murdoch became the drummer. He had never drummed before and was without any natural talent. I would sometimes drop by his house and hear him practising in a small room with the door closed. Few things are as angry sounding as a person learning to drum. Murdoch looked like someone in a band. He had spiky hair and the face of a Celtic street tough, and wanted to turn his poems into songs that made young women melt. The band practised in a garage, drank a lot of wine, and played around town. Like most bands, it flared briefly, then died.

After I moved east in 1981, I saw less of Murdoch, though he would sometimes come to Toronto and stay with me. I went to see him read his poetry at several Toronto venues, envious of this literary attention. At that point, I had published in a few small magazines and been rejected by a dozen larger ones. I had a job selling books for a publisher and drove a company car, a brown sedan. Sitting in the audience among all the dark poets like crows in their black jeans and jackets, I looked like Murdoch's parole officer. After his readings, he'd mingle with goth-looking girls in motorcycle jackets who approached to tell him they also wrote poetry and maybe he'd like to read some of it. And off they went.

Those were the days when the city was a network of rumour: a warehouse party where David Byrne might be, an absent-parent party at a Rosedale mansion, a speakeasy where Dan Aykroyd was drinking. We'd canvas the city for excitement, going to a rooftop party filled with poets and then off to see a punk band. We'd stagger out with ears buzzing, then head to a Queen Street bar to drink beer and wonder if the tattooed waitress had a boyfriend.

Murdoch was once flown out to Toronto to be a panellist on a television arts program—back in the era of big budgets and art as a going concern. The show was about

Leonard Cohen. Afterwards he was given a tape of the show and, when we got back to his hotel, he watched it. Murdoch was good on TV. I watched him watching himself. This was a high point in his life—on top of his game, flown to the big city and put up in a nice hotel. A lean, handsome man who liked a drink.

Early the following afternoon, he suggested grabbing a beer, though he warned, "I don't mind not starting, but I don't like stopping." His drinking had always been a concern, but when you're young, excessive drinking looks like exuberance. At some point—around thirty—it started to look like alcoholism, dull and grey and grinding. It took a toll. He had been supported by a succession of lovely, long-suffering women, but he'd exhausted their patience and love. He spiralled downward, drinking too much. Eventually he was broke and suffering, and tried to kill himself for the first time. His plan was to stab himself while in the shower so as not to make a mess, but he slipped and stabbed himself non-fatally.

Friends in the theatre world organized a benefit to help him out. They raised several thousand dollars, as much as he'd seen at any given time in his life. The idea was that it would help him get back on his feet, that he would quit drinking. He didn't quit and became increasingly difficult.

A friend whose car died one winter night knocked on his door. Murdoch answered, and the friend apologized for waking him up and asked if he could call him a cab. "You're a cab," Murdoch said and punched him in the face and slammed the door. He wrote less, drank more. At one point, he took a job on a landscaping crew and came into a party announcing, "Does it bother anyone that one of the country's best poets is *laying sod!*"

In his forties, despairing, he tried to kill himself by drinking more than his usual pail of vodka and sitting in a running car in a closed garage. It didn't work (he was thwarted by the catalytic converter), and he woke up poisoned and hungover.

He tried Alcoholics Anonymous but told me he wasn't really an AA guy. He wasn't interested in anyone else's story, for one thing, and he didn't believe in a higher power. The coffee sucked. And he didn't stop drinking. He went to a clinic in British Columbia to dry out, surrounded by skinny meth-head bikers. It wasn't a success, but he tried another program and eventually he did quit. He migrated to Vancouver Island, to a small town, and lost touch with most of the old gang, including me. Years slipped by. I heard he had throat cancer, was in a bad way, that he was back in Alberta, though few people had seen him. I thought he was one of those friends who quietly disappear from your life. You knew them way back when, then you lose touch and they're gone.

So it was a surprise one day when I received an email from him that included a photograph of an idyllic-looking pink house on a tropical coast. He was living in Bermuda, of all places. While recovering from cancer, he'd reconnected with a woman he'd known for years, and they fell in love. She was a lawyer who'd applied for the job of Crown counsel in Bermuda and, to her surprise, got it. They moved there, to the pink house on the ocean. Murdoch sent me a photograph of himself in a boat, wearing shorts, tanned, his hair blond in the sun. All of this was staggeringly incongruous. After a life of basement suites and black jeans and marginal employment, he was living the life of Riley.

Several years went by where he sent me emails that included pictures of egrets and sunsets and tropical flowers. He had stumbled into the most unlikely of second acts. A middle-aged man living the bourgeois life he had railed against for much of his youth. I often told his story as a lesson in redemption. Life was good in Bermuda, though his eyesight was failing, he wrote, the result of years of smoking and drinking or just inheriting his father's genes. He'd also lost part of his tongue to cancer and he had some trouble talking and could no longer taste anything.

Then the second act came to an abrupt end. He started drinking again, and it quickly went from heavy to disastrous. He couldn't write. His sight had gotten to the point where he couldn't recognize faces. He ranted and yelled and withdrew. He and his wife agreed he should spend some time back in Canada. He still had family in Calgary and it was his home, but the city was expensive and competitive and filled with sharp elbows. So he went back to Vancouver Island, where he was familiar with the medical and rehab system. He didn't like the small town he was in, described it as crappy, but didn't know where else to go. He quit drinking, started and quit again, financially supported by his wife, who had stayed in Bermuda. Then in January, he stepped in front of an eighteen-wheel truck, hoping to end his life. At that point, he was once again so out of touch with old friends that I didn't hear about it.

In April he sent me that email telling me about it, saying his eyesight was getting worse, that he found it extremely difficult to read. Books and newspapers were out of the question, emails a struggle. "I listen to books on tape and keep up as best I can with (the always grim) news but man o man it is hard." The next email arrived in the structure of a poem, whether by habit or the result of his failing eyesight or a computer formatting anomaly:

No excuse but my eyesight is bad
I still should be in touch more often
I was in the psych ward when I heard about Michael
[Michael Green, a mutual friend who was killed in a car
    accident]
And am still banged up from the suicide attempt.
I am hanging in best I can
And sending you
Best thoughts.

In the next email, he wrote, "I always found writing difficult but as my eyesight failed it just became too hard and so my whole sense of myself just tanked." However, he wrote, he would probably survive. "I suck at suicide, best efforts notwithstanding."

On his website, he wrote nostalgically about the sixties. Murdoch felt deeply connected to Kent State and Haight-Ashbury and Greenwich Village, the idea that a filament of politics and fashion and music had joined millions all across North America.

"I was a hurt young man," he wrote. "I duked it out of my childhood as best I could and I dragged a grief around with me I didn't even know I had. But you must remember (and you other old vets of that botched revolution do I am sure) our personal stories blended into the political one, even the historical one. For me, those years, say from 1968 through to about '73, were like watching the kids surfing in the bay here—just catch the wave and ride it. . . . I was a hurt young man and tender hearted but the times swept us up, each of us and flung us together randomly, often beautifully. All of it lived to a music beautiful to this day. We lived and we lived."

But that life was decades behind him, and now he was extraordinarily isolated. He still spoke to his wife regularly, but had contact with few people other than a therapist. What was left was the possibility of writing. "I feel like I have a book in me," he wrote to me in an email, "but as you know, even on a level playing field writing is a bitch, and blind and sad and often drunk and can't talk so pretty . . . Yikes."

He certainly had the material for a book. He didn't write it, though. He picked at the corners, writing entries on his website, a few poems.

I got one of his last emails a month later. I responded and he wrote a note saying it took ages just to read an email, to keep them short, but he would get back to me. In September a friend found him dead in his apartment.

I reread his emails and went to his website. On it he had written about the plight of the working class: bad teeth, less of everything—money, education, opportunities. "Almost everything conspires when one is born to the working class to beat the genius out of us."

He had held to the notion of his own genius for a long time. Perhaps he took it to his grave. It was one of the central buttresses of his life, though who knows what his heart held. "I study despair," he wrote on his blog. "It is part of my job."

It was his own despair that he studied. It was the closest, the most abundant and the most meaningful. His last months must have been ruled by it—in a small town, ailing, blind, drunk when possible, isolated.

A friend told me Murdoch had been dying for a long time. Decades, really. His poetry, like almost all poetry, was largely unheralded and only kept alive by his own attention to it. He reread himself with appetite. He called once to say he'd just gone through his oeuvre and that he "was pretty hot right out of the chute." He was a gifted teacher— charismatic, passionate about poetry and literature, deeply read—who could inspire others. He had a few chances to teach, but his lack of formal credentials and his own doubts did him in.

In *Dead Poets Society,* Robin Williams plays a teacher who exhorts his students to seize the day, telling them that as hard as it is to believe at the age of seventeen, they will wither and die, and before they do they will look back and examine the landscape that was their life. Did they live enough? Love enough? What did they leave? When Williams hanged himself at sixty-three, he left some brilliant performances and some sentimental kitsch, a remarkable talent overcome by darkness.

What Murdoch left were vivid memories of our youth, wine-filled, laughing. He'd had a gift for youth, but by forty, he talked of himself as a grizzled veteran of the art wars. Forty wasn't the new thirty for him, it was the new sixty. "I have learned," he wrote in his forties, "and probably too late, that life is not a poem. It is money and taxes and visits to the doctor and getting enough exercise and not smoking a zillion cigarettes and not drinking all the vodka in the world. Now here I am, forty-four years old, crinkly-faced from a zillion cigarettes, red-faced from all the vodka in the world and I realize that no poem in the world can save me."

———

In 2001, James Pennebaker, a psychology professor at the University of Texas, Austin, used a software program to compare three-hundred poems by eighteen famous poets, nine of whom had committed suicide. In the suicide camp were Sylvia Plath, Anne Sexton, Hart Crane, Randall Jarrell and others. The non-suicide control group included Lawrence Ferlinghetti (a favourite of Murdoch's), Adrienne Rich and Boris Pasternak.

"We found those who are suicidal use language very differently than those who are not suicidal," Pennebaker said. "The suicidal poets do not make reference to 'he,' 'she,' 'them,' or 'we.' They overuse 'I' almost as if they are unable to connect to others."

While Murdoch's poetry leaned heavily on first-person narrative, the "I" rarely far from it, Pennebaker's study may say more about the study of suicide than about poets. Put aside the tiny, subjective sample, and you are still left with a conceptual leap: that the use of the first-person pronoun suggests the writer is unable to "connect to others," that communicating your own experience may indicate a suicidal nature. Pennebaker's observation that "poets, as a group, are not the most chipper people on earth," is an understatement, though it doesn't offer much insight.

A 2003 study by psychologist James Kaufman with the

ominous title "The Cost of the Muse: Poets Die Young" noted that poets have the shortest life expectancy among writers—62.2 years (Murdoch died when he was 61.9). Kaufman thought the early deaths were likely linked to mental illness, given that poets were more introspective, poorer, more emotive and more vulnerable than most.

There has long been a link between creativity and suicide—the list is extensive (Yukio Mishima, Virginia Woolf, Sylvia Plath, Diane Arbus, Mark Rothko). A Swedish study from the Karolinska Institutet examined the data from 1.2 million people and showed that male artists were twice as likely to commit suicide as the general population.

The conclusion would seem to be that artists have a predilection to madness, in all its modern forms. The romantic interpretation is that art shows us a world we can't quite glimpse, and the explorers who take us there pay a price for that knowledge. But the Swedish researchers, who also noted a correlation between writers and alcoholism and mental illness, suggested an inverted causality—that those who are mentally ill turn to art as a form of therapy. That artists—some, at least—use art to self-medicate. If this is true, it poses an obvious problem. What happens when the medication is no longer effective—when your novel is panned or remains unwritten, your paintings unsold, your poetry neglected.

Who is happier in late middle age—the person who followed their bliss, who had some success and a modest profile as an artist but who didn't make a great living and whose later years are cramped and mean, or the guy who worked in the post office all his life and hated every minute but now has a decent pension and is taking up the guitar and going to Greece for the winter? It depends on when you talk to them. Art is not for the squeamish; it tends to favour the young.

Murdoch's last email to me ended with a poem-formatted paragraph.

> Rereading this I can see it is higgly piggly
> But you get my drift I hope
> I also hope you don't feel like you have to do something
>   . . .
> That is not the intention of these notes

I did feel like I should do something. Though I didn't. Before Murdoch succeeded in killing himself, I spoke to a mutual friend who'd also heard about his January suicide attempt, and we talked about what could be done. Murdoch lived thousands of kilometres away. Both of us were stressed—financially, professionally. We were busy with kids and schedules and work. Who could take in a blind man with a drinking problem. Would it help? What would his quality of life be? What would ours be? All this was posed as a philosophical issue. And then it wasn't, and my guilt crept in.

After he died, I reread his poetry. Selectively, it reads like a suicide note. "We will together be witness to my demise," he wrote in a poem when he was twenty-eight. "It is necessarily part of the experiment and like all scientists I am unafraid. Come with me and watch the art and the science take its toll. We will see nicotine stains and empty glasses. We will mark carefully the progress of my hairline and my gums. We will record memory loss and the decline of imaginative thought. We will watch my shaking hands."

That dark hole in the centre loomed. It looms in many of us. *What have I done with my life?* After you take that not-always-joyful inventory, there is the question: What is left to be done? What is possible? The answer isn't always uplifting. Murdoch was unable to write much of anything, let alone a novel. Small pleasures had disappeared from his life, and blindness had descended, his perpetual twilight soon to become total darkness.

What would I do if I knew I was going blind? My own eyes are getting better and worse at the same time. My distance vision is improving, a not uncommon thing, it turns out. I no longer need glasses to watch the biggish TV screen in the basement. But in the morning, my eyes refuse to focus to read the paper, which blurs and shifts. Sometimes ten minutes go by before I can check the scores, the first place I go to in the paper; a reflex—I no longer watch the games. Floaters scan across my eye in that odd, slo-mo amniotic march.

Blindness would be crushing, but I have children who still need me (more or less). I need them, at any rate. Without the anchor of family, who knows? I try to contemplate this scenario, then quickly abandon the morbid thought.

I flew out to Calgary for Murdoch's funeral. We gathered at his grave on an unseasonably warm October day, what would have been his sixty-second birthday. There was a dramatic western sky, a chinook arch pushing the clouds east. His youngest brother was there, an eerie replica of Murdoch. He was even dressed in black shirt, black suit jacket, blue jeans, black boots (Murdoch's boots, in fact). He stood there smoking a cigarette, creating the unsettling illusion that Murdoch was attending his own funeral.

The following evening a celebration of Murdoch's life was held in a theatre. The written testimonials ("Murdoch was a founding member of the alternative arts scene . . . the gift of himself he gave to so many of us is both precious and memorable") were still untainted by post-funeral sniping.

A large screen displayed a slide show of photographs as we listened to audio of Murdoch reading his poetry. The photographs—158 of them—ran by in a chronological scroll. It began with photos of a generic 1950s schoolboy. When he was a kid, Murdoch told me he sometimes went riding with his father through the foothills west of Calgary in the evenings. That land is now covered in suburbs and malls and car dealerships, but then it would have been beautiful, undulating countryside with stands of pines. Perhaps they saw one of those magical sunsets, the sun behind the mountains lighting up the underside of clouds in Technicolor reds.

It must have been grand, riding with his father, but most of his childhood wasn't grand.

The photographs moved from angelic schoolboy, through sullen early adolescent, the sudden hippie version at fifteen, the emerging poet—a beautiful young man— then the final segue to an unsmiling sixty-year-old who looked ambushed by age. It is the young version that is the most interesting (and a surprise to see my younger self in one of the photos). In those photos, Murdoch is laughing or defiant or pensive, always smoking, looking like a poet, still convinced of his impending greatness, the arc of many imagined lives.

11

SUICIDOLOGY

Each year there are dozens of suicide conferences, spread across the globe, often organized by a national association. Usually there is a theme (such as Mental Health and Human Resilience, The Silent Epidemic, Breaking Down Walls & Building Bridges). They offer speeches and seminars by suicidologists and support groups. I decided to go a conference in Niagara Falls, mostly because it was close to home, but also because the keynote speaker was David Lester, the most prolific suicidologist (author of ninety-nine books and 2,550 papers), one of the most esteemed and, at the time, the holder of the title Mr. Suicidology.

The original Mr. Suicidology was Edwin Shneidman (1918–2009), who coined the term. He wrote that suicide was the result of psychological pain, what he called "psychache." All other factors—depression, shame, hopelessness, debt, genetics—were pertinent in that they could lead to unbearable despair. "No one has to die," Shneidman was fond of saying. "It's the one thing that will be done for you."

The birth of modern suicidology came in 1949 at the Veterans' Administration neuropsychiatric hospital in West Los Angeles, where Shneidman was working as a clinical psychologist. He was asked to write condolence letters to the widows of two veterans who had taken their own lives. When he went to the county coroner's office to get the men's files, he discovered 721 suicide notes in a vault. He felt they could be a valuable research tool and took them (without permission). This wasn't, he wrote, the pivotal moment in a life that became devoted to the study of suicide. That came a few minutes later, "in the instant when [he] had a glimmering that their vast potential value could be immeasurably increased if [he] did *not* read them, but rather compared them, in a controlled blind experiment, with simulated suicide notes that might be elicited from matched nonsuicidal persons." This was, he said, "the golden road to suicide."

There have since been more than three hundred studies of suicide notes, yielding various, occasionally contradictory insights. People who die by suicide aren't always honest about why and, given their state, the writers don't necessarily offer metaphysical truths about life or poetic conclusions. A surprising number address practical matters ("Don't forget to feed the dog").

When Shneidman founded the Suicide Prevention Center in Los Angeles in 1955, it was to little notice. Suicide was under-reported and stigmatized. Society's interest, then as now, was mostly with celebrity suicides. In 1962, the profile of the institution was raised when it was brought in to help the city coroner determine if Marilyn Monroe had killed herself. Shneidman conducted what he termed a psychological autopsy on the troubled actress and determined that she had. A splashy start, but also something of a false start. During the following decade, the growth of the neurosciences and the growing power of the pharmaceutical industry outpaced Shneidman's psychological approach, and it was more difficult to get funding. It was the era of the magic bullet. The hope was that science would find the neurological cause of suicide and the pharmaceutical companies would develop a pill to prevent it, displacing psychology, which, to a degree, they have, in the form of widespread use of antidepressants. But Shneidman helped drag suicide out of the shadows into the light, where we can examine it.

————

Niagara Falls is a suicide magnet of sorts; each year between twenty and forty people die by suicide going over the Falls. The statistic's wide range is because it isn't always clear if ending up in the river was intentional or an accident, or even the act of a thrill seeker hoping to survive.

The conference I attended there was titled Stepping Out of the Darkness. I checked in at the hotel and went to the ballroom where David Lester was going to talk. It was filled with several hundred people—social workers, survivors of loss, psychologists, psychiatrists, sociologists.

A colleague introduced Lester with a lengthy speech that ended with his appellative, Mr. Suicidology, with its Vegas ring (*And now let's bring on with a big hand . . .*). When Lester finally took the microphone, he announced, "We really have no idea why people kill themselves."

It was a surprising, though refreshing, statement. Lester had an academic mien, a tweed jacket, a clipped beard, a soft British accent. He said he was less interested in a quantitative approach that searched for patterns—the groupings of dentists, doctors, people with depression, single people, and so on. He was turning to a qualitative approach. He had solicited journals of people who had died by suicide from their relatives and was examining them. Colleagues had developed a software program, an updated version of the software that James Pennebaker had used to analyze the verse of suicidal poets. They went through the journals and noted morbid references. In most cases, Lester said, the references lessened or even disappeared entirely as the person got closer to the act. The journals were pessimistic until the writers made the decision to kill themselves, then the tone brightened.

Lester talked about Arthur Inman, a reclusive, unsuccessful poet who took his own life in 1962. Inman left a seventeen-million-word journal, one of the longest in English. A two-volume version was published in 1986, which resulted in a play, *Camera Obscura,* and an opera titled *The Inman Diaries.* Inman had inherited wealth and didn't need to work, and he rarely left his apartment. Instead, the world came to him. He'd put an ad in the newspaper inviting people to come and tell him their stories for one dollar, and in the course of his life, he listened to roughly a thousand people—sailors, prostitutes, actresses, prizefighters, taxi drivers. He fell in love with some of them, had sex with some. This was his entire social world, his life. In the end, it wasn't enough, and Inman shot himself.

Wrapping up his talk, Lester asked, rhetorically, "What have we learned? I have no conclusion, no tidy ending. Perhaps nothing special happens, but one more grain of sand added to the pile results in the pile collapsing, and then we hold that grain of sand responsible for the collapse." It is the most sensible analysis of suicide I've run across.

I spent a few days at the conference, going to seminars on how the media handled suicide (not always delicately), on public suicide policy (underfunded), on new prevention strategies. After the conference, I sent Lester an email requesting an interview. I mentioned that my interest in suicide stemmed from my brother's death. He responded, "You don't want to talk to me. I'm seventy-two and cranky. You lost a brother to suicide. I am not a conventional suicidologist. I am full of eccentric ideas that would upset survivors."

I told him I wasn't easily upset and, after a few more emails, he agreed to talk on the phone. I called the next day and asked about his prodigious output, which seemed obsessive. "I am definitely obsessive," he said.

Lester told me that suicide rates are an index of quality of life. Though it isn't when times are difficult that suicides go up—it's when things are good. "You'd think suicide rates would go down when things are good and up when things are harder," he said. "But when things are good, you can no longer blame outside forces for your problems. You internalize it—it must be you."

Ireland had a spike in suicides during the 1990s, when

the Celtic Tiger was running wild and the country's sleepy economy suddenly boomed. In the transition from a traditional society to a modern one, the shared values that had bound the Irish were eroded, but new values hadn't yet been created to replace them. This, at least, was the explanation offered by sociologists. The economic juggernaut produced winners and losers in a society that, if the national literature is anything to go by, had been uniformly miserable. So the good times were more difficult to bear, in part because they weren't shared.

Yet in Calgary, which had an extraordinary oil boom in the seventies, the opposite happened. During the decade-long boom, the suicide rate was low. When the economy crashed in 1982, there were 5,444 calls to the suicide hotline at the suicide prevention centre, more than double the figure in the previous year (2,262), which had been the height of the boom.

This is one of the difficulties with studying suicide. There are few universal truths; the circumstances that drive one individual toward suicide have the opposite effect on another. David's suicide came when things looked to be going well for him at last, at least from the outside.

Lester's point about good times is supported by statistics. A 2010 article on suicide in *Scientific American* noted, "Most people who kill themselves actually lived better-than-average lives. Suicide rates are higher in nations with higher standards of living than in less prosperous nations; higher in US states with a better quality of life; higher in societies that endorse individual freedoms; higher in areas with better weather; in areas with seasonal change, they are higher during warmer seasons; and they're higher among college students that have better grades and parents with higher expectations." Suicide has less to do with our circumstances than with our expectations.

Lester used to publish a compendium of suicide research every decade, but he ceased doing it once the digital revolution took hold. "Everything is on the Internet now—a hundred thousand articles," he said. "But researchers only look at the most recent work. Few people go back any farther. So we are repeating ourselves. We reinvent the wheel because we no longer know what's been done. The research is better, the data is better now, statistical analysis is better." But researchers tend to cover the same perplexing territory over and over.

I asked Lester if he would continue his study in retirement. "I'm quitting cold turkey," he said. "I've already given all the books away. I'm putting it all behind me."

———

I wish I could do the same, but it's as if David's death opened up a conversation that millions are quietly having (sometimes with themselves) and I can't stop listening in. Among Lester's many academic papers are studies of artists and suicide. One of them, titled "An Analysis of Poets and Novelists Who Completed Suicide," noted that a study of thirty members of the writer's workshops at the University of Iowa showed that 80 percent had "an affective disorder," 30 percent abused alcohol, and two of the writing faculty had committed suicide.

In a sample of thirteen writers who had taken their own lives, all but one had either depression or alcoholism (the lone exception had schizophrenia). In another study, Lester looked at writers in several different countries—Britain, Russia, Japan and the United States—all of whom had high incidences of suicide, an occupational rather than cultural phenomenon.

And it's only getting worse for writers. For decades I wrote for magazines and newspapers, two entities that are slowly fading as the world goes digital. Their rates haven't budged much in twenty-five years. The book business doesn't offer much respite. A colleague, an award-winning novelist, had tried (unsuccessfully) to get a job as a bike courier in his fifties. He said he realized that his work was kept alive solely by the force of his personality; when he went, it would too. And he almost did go, surviving a suicidal bout that saw him hospitalized. But he recovered and said his depression had been like "a foreign country, a sunless and hostile place." A friend who had been long-listed for the Man Booker Prize told me he was thinking of becoming an Uber driver. Publishing is in turmoil, and a generation is growing up on social media. My agent has told various clients that literary fiction is dead. She's not alone in this view; she describes her job these days as managing a crisis hotline as much as making book deals.

This conversation has been going on for twenty years, maybe two hundred years, it's true. We have always been complaining, pining for a golden era that may or may not have existed. And the death of the novel has been predicted for generations now, though it somehow keeps limping along. But the current crisis feels existential. It is certainly more difficult to make a living. There are more options (online, self-publishing), but fewer resources. More books, less money. An agent recently told a friend who pitched a novel that she should write it for herself. Writing is becoming a hobby.

Two blocks from my house, there is a used bookstore that is run by a reclusive man. He wears pants that are cut off below the knees, in a jagged Robinson Crusoe fashion. The books are mostly scavenged from people's recycling bins. The store is never open. When I walked past once, I saw him sitting at a small desk, sipping a huge drink. There were fast-food containers all over the floor. I tried the door, but it was locked. He looked at me like a hunted animal. And there are black days when I think that this is the future of publishing.

There is a bridge near my house where more than four hundred people have jumped. The Bloor Viaduct was built in 1918 and soon became part of a global tradition of suicide bridges; San Francisco's Golden Gate Bridge has had sixteen hundred jumpers, China's Nanjing Yangtze River Bridge, two thousand. Most countries seem to have one such spot. The viaduct is a pleasant ten-minute walk from my house, across a lovely park, along a street of heavily mortgaged homes. Dozens of writers live in my neighbourhood, so perhaps it was only a matter of time before these two statistical probabilities collided.

A writer who lived two blocks away from me, H.S. Bhabra, was one of the last people to jump before the city put up a protective steel veil to prevent jumping. A week before his forty-fifth birthday, Bhabra stepped off the bridge, landing fifty-five metres below on the concrete of the Bayview extension. The headline that appeared after his death was "Failed Writer Commits Suicide." How do you define "failed writer"?

His first novel, *Gestures,* won an award, but he had trouble following it up. He was writing the Big Novel—a four-part opus—but was blocked. And he was broke. He was living with a woman he owed twenty-five thousand dollars to, and they shared a house with a mutual friend, a physicist. On May 31, 2000, the physicist was walking to the subway and saw Bhabra standing outside the local library, smoking a cigarette. He found out later that Bhabra was taking a break from writing a dozen or so suicide letters—one of them to the physicist himself. They waved to each other.

Bhabra finished writing the letters ("By the time you read this . . ."), then mailed them. In the early morning, he walked to the bridge, climbed onto the wide stone railing and looked at the view. The sun would have been just over the horizon, the traffic light. The valley was green and undisturbed. It was a view that hundreds of desperate people had pondered before him. He jumped.

I went to visit Vee Ledson, the woman who had lived with Bhabra. She still lived nearby and was now married to Allan Randall, the physicist roommate. They sat on the couch across from me, telling the story of their lost friend. In his suicide note to Vee, Bhabra admitted, "There was no book. I didn't write it." He had told a friend that *Gestures* hadn't gotten the reception it deserved (the natural view of most novelists). He made up two lists of the top hundred books of all time: one for books in English, the other an international list. On the English list, *Gestures* was number two, behind *Catch-22*. On the international list, a modest eighth.

This was delusional, yet how different was Bhabra's mental state from that of thousands of other artists? While I am working on a book, I imagine its sweeping power. Unfinished, or better yet, unwritten, it has an undisturbed magnificence. Once into the project, I tenuously hang on to these fantasies, while at the same time fighting crippling doubt (Is it limp, is it *alive?*). In my head, I simultaneously hold these antithetical versions of my work and, by extension, myself. F. Scott Fitzgerald said the test of a first-rate intelligence is the ability to hold two opposing ideas in your mind and still function. But most people, and certainly most writers, hold two versions of themselves in their head all the time—the one that is rooted (and restrained) by reality, and the one that takes flight. And we function. Perhaps that's why we function. Faced only with reality, we'd be crippled.

Randall told me, "Bhabra failed to become the person he had imagined when he was in his twenties. And at forty-four, he felt there wasn't enough time left to become that person."

We all construct a version of our future selves, perhaps not consciously or meticulously, but no teenager leaves high school dreaming of minimum-wage drudgery, love-lessness and a long commute. No one dreams of becoming a marginalized writer. But the tiny defeats accumulate—a mean-spirited review, mild sales, insufficient acclaim—accentuated by the success of others. *How the hell did X win the Booker Prize?* A series of small steps bring us to a middle age that is mired in disappointment. The writer Charles Bukowski observed that most of us are finished by twenty-five. "We are like roses that have never bothered to bloom when we should have bloomed," he wrote, "and it is as if the sun has become disgusted with waiting."

In his note to Ledson, Bhabra wrote, "Only magic could have saved me and I can no longer rely on magic." Many of us rely on magic of some kind, whether it's religion or art or our own magical thinking. It brings comfort and, occa-sionally, meaning. When it fails us, we lose our faith and we can no longer sustain the idea that our lives are other than what they are.

Writing has always been a precarious way to make a living, but now it is joined by dozens of jobs that used to be as safe as houses. Which are themselves no longer safe. During the great recession of 2008–2009, boomers were hardest hit by lost property value and retirement savings. Twenty-seven percent of people aged fifty to sixty-four experienced a reduction in their salaries, more than any other age group. In a follow-up study to her original suicide research, Julie Phillips looked at whether recent boomer suicides were due to personal (mental health), interpersonal (divorce), or external (economic) circumstances. External was the one area that showed an increase.

Middle-aged white males have the highest rate of suicide. In the United States, the only racial group that is close is Native Americans. The study concluded that white people are less used to adversity and aren't adjusting well. Native Americans have suffered generations of racism and poverty and experienced a dispossession that is unrivalled. While there is a wide economic gap between the two groups, and little historic commonality, white men appear to be approaching a sense of dispossession from another perspective. In both groups, there is a dearth of hope. One group fears it might not get better; the other fears it will only get worse. When I look at my brother and those friends who killed themselves, I think they felt dispossessed, unable to imagine a place for themselves in this world.

12

FAR FROM HOME

Almost a decade after David's death, I was back in Calgary, helping my parents move into their new, much smaller condo. A chinook arch cut across the western sky, the air warm for January. A few people were outside in shirtsleeves. My father and I were driving to Home Depot to pick up framing hooks, light bulbs, L-brackets—a list of things they needed for the new place. His memory was fading and he talked about its limitations. He sounded disappointed by it, like it was a child he'd expected more from.

In the car, he turned to me and asked, "What made your brother do what he did?"

It was a question he'd been asking himself over the years. I didn't have an answer, only the various narratives I'd been struggling with myself.

"I don't know, Dad. He was unhappy he lost Anna Mae, unhappy about a lot of things." I said drugs had been a part of it, and the fact that middle age arrived like an intruder, that he'd somehow felt isolated. My father nodded, the answer too vague for his logical mind.

"When did we know?" he asked.

"We didn't." We didn't know he was edging toward a cliff. We were too far away, though even those who saw him every day didn't know.

"I went through all our photographs," he said. "You never see David smiling. Even as a boy."

"You think he was always depressed?"

"Maybe. Maybe it's something he always had inside him."

This was my father's logical brain at work, a man who'd once gotten 100 percent on a calculus exam in university. The reason needed to be something identifiable, something tangible.

We got to Home Depot and wandered the aisles. My grandfather owned a hardware store, and my father has a lifelong love of such places. All that utility—loose nails, tools, rope. A place where practical men kept the world intact with duct tape and wood screws. We trudged the concrete floor. The man we asked for help, not much younger than my father, had a battered drinker's face. The job was a new start, perhaps.

While my father struggled with his short-term memory, his childhood memories were extraordinarily vivid. On our way back from the store, Dad recalled his earliest memory, a near-death experience. It was 1934, and he was four years old, suffering from double pneumonia. "My mother had been a nurse," he said. "I was white as a sheet and had a high fever and she knew what it was, but neither Fort Frances nor International Falls had a hospital. My mother thought she was going to lose me. There was only one taxi driver in town and she called him. She told him she wanted to go to Duluth [in Minnesota, 160 miles and a border away]. It was snowing and the guy didn't know how to get there, but he drove south and somehow got to Duluth and found the hospital, which my mother thought was due to divine guidance. The doctors treated me and when I got home, I remember sitting in bed. I'd lost weight, and my mother and Aunt Gladys were hovering over me, and Gladys said, 'He looks like a plucked chicken.'"

Fort Frances, where he grew up, was a pulp-and-paper town that was often plagued by a distinctive rotting smell that came from its own mill and the one across the river in International Falls, Minnesota. It was a tough town, but it was also orderly and prim and had the kind of white picket fence sensibility you'd see in a Jimmy Stewart movie. My father and his two brothers had all grown up there and they escaped the mill, heading off to American universities. I had seen home movies of them from the 1940s, along with black and white photographs, and their childhoods seemed mythic to me.

While they were all happy to escape the mill, they remembered the town fondly, retailed the anecdotes and the Runyonesque names of local characters (Red Rippenbark, Snake Hoopchuk, Tooley Kawulia). Fort Frances had formed them.

My father still kept in touch with his childhood friends and had remained close to both of his brothers. They were the kind of brothers you saw on shows like *Bonanza,* with a tight bond occasionally fuelled by argument. They argued about politics, about American exceptionalism (his brother Don lived in Minneapolis), about single malt scotch. They were each other's best man when they got married, had all become professors. My father and his brother Don were sometimes mistaken for each other. I wonder if my father was disappointed that my brother and I hadn't replicated that intimate relationship. We were never the Hardy Boys, and I felt guilty that it was my fault.

Families change with each generation like the turn of a kaleidoscope, new patterns forming. The nineteenth-century version with nine kids gives way to the twenty-first-century version with one. Three generations are rooted on the farm and the fourth takes flight, never to return. We rise and fall, and mostly we adapt. My family had re-formed around David's absence the way a war vet adapts to a missing limb.

The next day my parents and I drove out to Banff for lunch. We ate at a place across the street from a bar where David's band used to play. The sun was out, the snowy mountains lit up. On the way back, we stopped to look at our old house, on the acreage west of Calgary.

The setting is spectacular, 320 acres of land shared by fifteen families, the houses situated along the ridge that was once used as a buffalo jump by the Blood Tribe (Kainai First Nation). The Rockies are visible to the west, a jagged white line marching south. Today they seemed closer than usual, an optical trick. We sat in the long driveway, not getting out of the car.

My parents lived here for almost thirty years before moving into Calgary, when the commute became too much. I lived here for only a few years, yet it is the place that feels most like home, the place I returned to. The landscape helps, that big sky, the mountains looming. The old Highway 1 crests just east of where our house was so that that you suddenly see the whole Bow Valley below and the mountains shining to the west, and when I drive out there and that vista opens up, something visceral tugs at me. My sister won't come out here. She tears up, the sense of home overwhelming her.

The new owner had built a gazebo and a dozen birdhouses and little monuments that cluttered my father's original pristine aesthetic. It felt a little like an unsuccessful yard sale.

I had worked on the construction of the house during a summer when I was going to university, framing it under the auspices of a gloomy Danish alcoholic. He rarely spoke and smoked hand-rolled cigarettes as he sullenly hammered away. The house was built on a steep hill, cantilevered into the forest. Every two days or so, the Dane would remark that there wasn't much point in finishing the place; it would slide down the hill and end up in the creek below. He knew my father had designed it. He drank vodka at lunch and looked like a figure from a Breughel painting.

A local guy named Paul helped out, a man in his early twenties who told me he'd been hit by lightning once. He was hit again that summer. We were working on another house that sat exposed on the ridge facing west, nailing down the plywood floor for the second storey. You could see the weather coming from forty miles away, dark clouds gliding toward us. When the clouds got close, lightning forking down to the ranchland, we climbed down and took cover. Except Paul.

"A little rain never hurt anyone," he said.

"A little lightning might, you halfwit," the foreman said. "Get the hell down from there."

He didn't, and lightning struck the house and Paul was knocked unconscious, his false teeth skittering across the subfloor. I remember being surprised that a guy so young had false teeth. He recovered and came back to work two weeks later, and tried, unsuccessfully, to think of a nickname for himself based on lightning never striking twice.

When our house was finished, it became a refuge and a social hub that was often filled with people. At a faculty party one night, one of the professors, who was originally from Brooklyn, looked out the floor-to-ceiling windows into the forest and saw a bobcat. "There's a lion out there," he said. David's band regularly practised in the family room because no other parents would let them play in their houses. They'd play music, go outside and smoke a joint, then sit in the sauna my father and I had built.

My ten-year-old sister got a horse, a stubborn beast we bought from a neighbouring rancher for fifty bucks. She would ride it in the bowl to the south that had been gouged by a glacier millennia ago. I was going to university, and David was in the high school I had just left. The city was filled with families that had come to take advantage of the oil boom, had uprooted themselves to find a new life here in the West. And their children were dropping acid in the high-school washroom and hot-knifing hash on their parents' stoves and smoking a joint before physics class because they believed it helped them understand the universe, and David was at the forefront of this Age of Discovery.

The idea, oft debated by my brother, that pot was less harmful than alcohol, that he wasn't hurting anyone by smoking the odd joint, that half of North America was stoned at least some of the time, met with something approaching a weary acceptance by my parents. It was a liberal household, and my father worked with university students who were smoking pot and may have tried it himself on one of the mountain retreats the Environmental Design faculty used to go on (he came back from one and explained to me how a roach clip worked). But whatever grudging tolerance for David's pot habit existed came to an abrupt end when he got caught selling a pound of dope to an undercover RCMP officer. The fact that a clever, expensive lawyer managed to get him off was a huge relief to my parents, but it also stamped an indelible criminality on what had been merely a pastime. From both a legal and parental perspective, there was a wide gap between smoking a joint during band practice and being branded a drug dealer. They'd had a sudden, wrenching glimpse of another life for my brother, a life that was far from the life in that house.

Our dog, Cream, a lab/shepherd mix, tried to kill herself here. She used to come out for walks with whoever was going. One winter my father took her down to Jumping Pound Creek, which was frozen, and she skittered along the ice, then fell through, plunging into the water. My father pulled her out, but she was too arthritic to walk and he had to carry her back, a long walk with a heavy dog. Over the next few weeks, she became stiffer and more limited, and she finally limped into the forest behind the house, dug a place for herself in the snow and lay down to die. We tracked her through the snow and found her and brought her home, worried that the magpies or coyotes would get at her when she was still alive but too weak to fend them off. But she went back a few days later. She knew it was her time. The Roman philosopher Seneca said the wise man "lives as long as he ought, not as long as he can." Animals sense this, but most humans still prize quantity over quality. After carrying her back from the forest again, we took Cream to the vet in town and had her put to sleep, that gentle euphemism that only applies to pets. Decades later, my sister and I still occasionally dream about her.

One of the houses I worked on out on the shared property belonged to a painter, who died "suddenly" at the age of seventy-four. It was a suicide, we heard. He was a talented artist. My parents owned one of his paintings, a moody landscape that I liked. I'd hung it on the wall in their new condo the day before.

The houses we lived in had a mathematical symmetry: from the modest house in Wildwood, to the larger house nearby on a larger piece of land, then finally out here to an even larger house on hundreds of acres. And then my parents' gradual downsizing, first to a large condo in the city, then to a much smaller one. This was the rough arc for many of my parents' generation. This house had been their apex.

That night at dinner we talked about David. My mother said she'd heard his voice that December when he disappeared, while we still held out hope that he'd be in touch at Christmas. She was lying in bed, in that trance state before waking, not quite dreaming, and she heard him say, "I won't be coming home."

"I knew he was dead," she said.

She thought David just didn't want a normal life, with its tedious daylight hours, a wife he didn't love, a job that didn't thrill, a life familiar to millions but unfamiliar to him. It was the fate he had rebelled against, and it suddenly loomed.

Going through the moving boxes the next day and sorting CDs, we found one of an early band of David's called BOS (Bag of Shit, named for their fondness for pot). It was marked 1978, when he was just starting out. We put it on. They were playing bluegrass tunes, a cover of Ricky Nelson's "Hello Mary Lou," and a few instrumental compositions of David's. The sound was murky and uneven, but the musicianship was crisp. I could pick out David's banjo and piano. Between two songs, I heard David's voice and his distinctive laugh. It was both comforting and a bit unsettling, his presence suddenly in the room. I could picture him at the recording session—smell the pot and beer, hear the laughter, him living in the moment, all that possibility in the air.

"It's nice to hear his laugh," my mother said.

———

The following night I had dinner with a group of old friends. Most of us were in the arts, and the hunger for everything that defined us for so long had faded, the sexual frenzy long past us. These were people I loved, people who had been lovers. Everyone was hunkered down now with a reliable partner. We were joined by affairs, minor betrayals, a long parade of good times—though we all had our separate versions. Such is the power of art. When it comes to memory, everyone is an artist.

We talked about suicide, though in another context. Some of the group had parents who had had protracted deaths, their quality of life poleaxed. What about our own exits? Everyone agreed that when we got to the point when our quality of life had sufficiently frayed, we'd end it. A few said they were getting their kit in Mexico—Nembutal or "death in a bottle," sold in pet pharmacies there, a favourite of death tourists. One friend said his father had watched his own father suffer through dementia and a difficult death and told him, "You don't have to worry about me. I'm going to have a bottle of gin and a bottle of pills." When the time was right, he'd take both of them and just slip away. Though he didn't. He came home one night with a bag filled with gin and stumbled and fell and broke the bottles, injuring himself. He eventually moved from the hospital to an assisted living residence where his dementia blossomed. Oddly, he forgot he was an alcoholic, though he remembered his drink—a martini made with Beefeater gin and two olives—and would order it when in a restaurant, then forget to drink it. A lifelong habit nullified, a painless withdrawal. Though his withdrawal from life was protracted. So, a conundrum. When you're still of sound enough mind to take your own life, maybe you want to live, to hang on to those last moments, to take one more drink. Then you linger, until you no longer have the ability to make a decision about anything, let alone ending your life.

So whom do we appoint to do that for us? And how far gone do we need to be? for ourselves? for our loved ones? And does the same deadline apply to both? One friend said that his threshold was when he could no longer get to the bathroom on his own. We all have our tipping points—if we can't see, can't reason, can't move, can't enjoy a glass of wine.

Tanya, the youngest of us, said, "I'll take care of it for you. I'll give you the happiest hour of your life, then bang."

A tall order on both counts. A chorus of male voices: "You mean you'll have sex with us?"

"I'm going to contract that part out."

"You'll just kill us."

"How will you know we're ready? We lose our keys two days in a row and we're toast?"

A shrug. "I'll know."

Plato thought suicide was wrong because it released our souls from our bodies, which the gods had placed us in as a form of punishment. There are days when it feels the gods have done just that. But Plato made several exceptions, among them, "when the self-killing is compelled by extreme and unavoidable personal misfortune."

All of us had experienced unavoidable personal misfortune. Who hasn't? But misfortune is a broad category. Our loose, wine-fuelled fatal plans had less to do with misfortune, which you can sometimes see beyond, than with disease and incapacity, where there is no beyond.

In his book *Being Mortal,* Atul Gawande writes, "The body's decline creeps up like a vine. Day to day, the changes can be imperceptible. You adapt. Then something happens that finally makes it clear that things are no longer the same." He was talking about old age and infirmity, but a version of this applies to middle age, and to my brother's suicide. He had a house, friends, arguably the best job of his career outside of music. A fresh start, yet he'd felt cornered. There were options: divorce, a loan, a therapist, though a friend had said he wasn't the kind of guy who asked for help. But that isn't the future he would have seen. The future he saw was dark, inalterable.

Pete, David's former bandmate, told me, "The one thing I know for certain is that David feared growing old." Pete had already dealt with several serious health issues. "I cannot, for the life of me, imagine that Dave would have put up with any of that. Growing old is hard, and Dave didn't like to do anything that didn't come easy."

Music had come easily, perhaps too easily. David hadn't practised the piano for hours every day under the tutelage of a demanding teacher. He'd picked up new instruments and solved their mysteries without much effort: banjo, guitar, bass guitar, mandolin, harmonica, even oddities like the dulcimer. "The artist is nothing without the gift," Émile Zola said, "but the gift is nothing without work."

A year earlier, I'd returned to Calgary to attend the funeral service of a friend who died unexpectedly of a heart attack. Richard was a composer and sound designer who worked in theatre. We were exactly the same age, born only hours apart, and each year we exchanged emails on our birthday, assessing health, life and relationships. "MUST quit smoking," he wrote on our fifty-seventh birthday. At fifty-nine, he wrote, "Life is very good." He had just married his longtime partner, a prominent Mexican actress, and he sent photos of them holding hands and falling backward into the pool at their house in Mexico City. He had a few minor health complaints—dental issues, some back pain. He hadn't seen a doctor in years, but was thinking of finally getting a colonoscopy. Weeks after his sixtieth birthday, he was seized with a sudden, acute chest pain. He called 911, then collapsed during the call. He was on a land line and they traced it to the address, and paramedics broke down the door. Doctors and paramedics worked on him for hours, getting a pulse and losing it. And then he was gone.

I flew to Calgary for the service, seeking the comfort of the tribe. Hundreds of friends and relatives gathered in the downtown theatre space where he'd worked. After the service there was a wake at the house where Richard had collapsed, and I drove there with a friend I hadn't seen in a decade. We moved slowly through evening traffic in the dying light, and my friend told me about his depression. It wasn't like being depressed *about* something, he said, about marriage or money or work. It was something blacker, an inchoate cloud that enveloped him. He couldn't trust his own judgment. He'd closed the garage door, got in his car and turned on the engine. He was discovered semi-conscious and taken to emergency. Now he was healthy and cautious, running a company, doing well.

At the wake, we all drank and cried and caught up. Richard and I had loved the same woman at the same time, and were joined by that, oddly, rather than divided (though there were a few bumps along the way). On our twenty-fifth birthday, he'd bought me a bottle of scotch. Around the neck was a ribbon that held an earring. The idea was we would drink the scotch and then he'd pierce my ear. He had several earrings. We drank the scotch, but my ear remained intact; it was too big a leap for me.

I was sleeping on the couch in my parents' condo, not well, my dreams morbid and fractured. I woke up at a little after 5 a.m. when it was starting to get light. David's book of remembrance was on the coffee table, left there by my mother for me to look at. This was the first time I'd seen it. I picked it up and opened it to a photo of David standing at the summit of Abbot Pass at Lake O'Hara in the mountains. He's wearing sunglasses, smoking a joint, ironically holding a small Union Jack flag, Hillary reaching the peak of Everest. It's 1974 and his hair is past his shoulders. His nickname at the lodge where he worked was Princess. One of his friends had written, "Dave was a guy who liked to live in the moment." There was a quote from the Walt Whitman poem "When Lilacs in the Dooryard Bloom'd." The poem was written for Abraham Lincoln but applied chillingly to my brother. "I fled forth to the hiding receiving night that talks not, down to the shores of the water."

I opened my laptop and went to Google Earth and typed in David's old address in Whitehorse. There was his house. It was summer, incredibly green. Clouds splayed across a blue sky, distorted by the camera. I followed the empty road away from his house. Each click took me farther down the street in a staccato burst. I switched to satellite mode, pulling away, the roofs visible at first, then finally only a black and white grid seen from space, an abstraction. The distance between his house and the Marsh Lake Bridge a matter of inches.

I flew home to Toronto in the evening, watching a dumb movie, drinking wine from a plastic cup. My taste in film deteriorates with every foot of altitude gained. On planes I happily watch films I wouldn't watch on television, let alone in a theatre. Bring me your explosions, your saccharine love stories, your comedies that make Jerry Lewis look like Kierkegaard. Keep your art and bring me stupid relief in those hours suspended above it all.

13

THE SONG REMAINS
THE SAME

In my childhood, the snow came as early as October, threatening Halloween, every costume disguised by a winter coat. Winnipeg was winter, the self-proclaimed coldest city on the continent. In January the radio occasionally informed us that it was colder than Mars. My brother and I built snow forts, but the point of them was only in the building, like one of those Depression-era make-work projects for the unemployed. Once it was finished, all you could do was huddle inside, getting colder, boredom descending immediately.

Boredom was the great enemy of my brother's childhood. *There's nothing to do.* A constant refrain, in the house, in the car. When my brother got fidgety, my parents sent us outside and told us to run around the block. We'd wander the neighbourhood, looking for adventure, or go to the Wildewood Club (the *e* added in a British flourish) and rearrange the letters on the corrugated board at the entrance. If it announced a cocktail party for the Ladies Badminton Club, it would become "Bad Ladies and Cocks 5 pm." David keeping watch while I scrambled the letters to come up with something wicked, the adrenaline racing through us both.

School was boring, reciting poems from memory and the times table, many of the teachers stern and elderly. David inherited all of them after me, three years older and even sterner. In Sunday school, we memorized the books of the Old Testament in order and read cryptic passages out loud ("So Satan went forth from the presence of the Lord . . ."). But it was the United Church, a leisurely religion that was short on catechism, and our teacher, a tall, unpious man, once wrote on the blackboard "Tiger Cats/ Lions," the two teams then vying for football's Grey Cup. He ran through the relative strengths of each team and asked us who God would root for. He filled the bewildered silence with the answer: The Lions, who were, like us, from the West, which was God's country.

Church was even more boring than Sunday school, and on occasion we found ourselves sitting on the hard pews, singing the tuneless hymns, the minutes doled out painfully. The English metaphysical poet John Donne thought suicide may be a way to forgo the weariness of this life and more quickly get to the joys of the next one. But we weren't concerned with the afterlife, and neither was the rest of the congregation; their lives on earth were humming along.

We undertook short-lived hobbies, thrust upon us by a well-meaning uncle. A stamp collecting kit ("Watch your collection grow with you!") and rock collecting ("Be a rockhound for life!"). We had a mammoth model train set, incredibly intricate, handed down by a colleague of my father's. There was some kind of solution you could put in the locomotive so it blew steam. My father built a platform out of plywood and together we created a miniature world for trains. When it was finally done, the plywood painted in greens and blues for grass and lakes, we watched the first train go along that lengthy track, taking the corners, labouring up the inclines created by the orange plastic trestles. Diminishing returns set in immediately. What was the point? The train ran efficiently and uneventfully. We tried running over toy soldiers carefully laid across the track, but the train simply pushed them away. Like the snow forts, the fun was all in the construction. Once built, it disappointed.

I almost died of boredom. People say it all the time, a descriptive for their day at the office, a dinner party, a first date, that experimental play. Psychiatrists have developed clinical categories to describe it: psychodynamic boredom (you don't know what you want); attentional (you can't focus on what you want); sub-optimal arousal (you crave more stimulation than you're getting); existential (life is without meaning); dissociative disorder (you feel detached from the world). My brother could likely have ticked off a few of these, but millions could tick off at least one, probably more.

Music was the cure for David's boredom, which was epic in childhood and became an enemy in adulthood that he never entirely defeated. The music we played at our piano lessons—the scales and exercises and annoying, unfamiliar songs—wasn't really music. It was closer to math, a series of technical steps you needed to take to yield a product you weren't that interested in. Real music came from the radio. We lay in bed at night, our transistor radios under our pillows, a single hearing bud in our ear as we listened to CKRC. Our shared bedroom was a mirror image, with beds on opposite sides and two desks in the middle. The Top 40 in the sixties was a mélange of competing genres, and we lay there in the dark, hungry for certain songs, dreading others. You could hear the Doors' "Touch Me" followed by Leapy Lee ("Little Arrows"), then the Beatles (pick one). There were still unfortunate traces of the old guard (Sammy Davis singing "The Candy Man") and the occasional wretched oddity (Andy Williams singing "Battle Hymn of the Republic"). The culture was still at war with itself, and music was the most prominent battlefield.

The music had its own appeal, but part of the allure was the fact that as my brother and I lay there listening to "Penny Lane" and "Strawberry Fields" being played in succession, with an explanation about how the songs reflected the childhoods of Paul McCartney and John Lennon, respectively, we knew that thousands of other kids were listening to these same songs in our city. Millions more listened to their own snappy disc jockeys play the same songs in other cities. We were members of a larger club that we couldn't have defined at that age—but we could feel it. Music provided a connection not just to the outside world, but also to some unexplored part of my adolescent self.

We sometimes cycled the mile or so to Ringer's drugstore to buy Beatles cards, which came with bubble gum. They featured a photograph of one or more Beatles on the front, with questions and answers on the back. ("With all your good fortune, do you remember how it feels to be sad?" George: "I know I speak for all the boys when I say that we feel sad pretty often.") At the time, there was a certain pressure among friends to declare a favourite Beatle. I avoided Paul as too obvious and settled on George, the mysterious one. David went with John. We bought the cards and listened to the 45s, and David already had a Beatlesque haircut. We used to go to an art school on Saturdays, and when a kid showed up to class one day wearing a Beatle wig, I recognized instantly that this was a step too far in the Beatlemania sweepstakes. He did too, and before the class was over, he'd tossed the wig into the large garbage bin, where it sat like a dead crow.

When FM arrived, I slowly gravitated toward its hushed late-night tones. Banished were the sunny sounds of the Monkees and the Turtles. Instead I lay on the living room floor listening to the Doors, Jim Morrison going on about something deep. My mother examined my limited record collection and said, "I don't know why they can't come up with better names. And he's singing out of key."

David would sit at the piano and quickly figure out a song he'd just heard on the radio, the Stones or the Animals. His tastes grew more eclectic, and he would play Scott Joplin rags or rip through a twelve-bar blues, and later, Tom Waits tunes, singing in his gravelly voice. I had long since quit piano without any regrets, and hearing David practise a Chopin nocturne didn't change that. But once David started playing the familiar, thrilling chords of "Let's Spend the Night Together," I immediately realized the potential of the piano and was crushed once more by my lack of talent.

When it comes to suicide, musicians don't fare much better than writers. A study conducted at the University of Sydney examined a sample of 13,195 musicians who had died between 1950 and 2014. They found that these musicians had a life expectancy that was, on average, a shocking twenty-five years shorter than the general population's, and had suicide rates that were three times higher.

Instead of sex, drugs and rock and roll, the sociological battle cry was, sex, drugs, failed rehabilitation, bitterness, and early death. Certainly it's a precarious way to make a living, but successful musicians don't fare any better; the median age at death for musicians who had achieved some level of fame was only 45.2 for North American musicians and 39.6 for European musicians. The data was interesting and exhaustive, but no real conclusion was reached. "We can only speculate about the potential causes of these results. . . . Popular musicians as an occupational group are highly vulnerable to the vagaries of their workplaces and their inherent personal vulnerabilities."

The vagaries of the workplace include playing in places where drugs and alcohol are abundant, and where people tend to offer you both. The inherent personal vulnerabilities are harder to pin down, and David hid his vulnerabilities brilliantly.

A study that examined mortality rates for musicians by genre showed that hip hop, rap, metal and punk musicians were at greatest risk, with metal musicians claiming the highest suicide rate (a staggering 19.3 percent, roughly one per band). Oddly, the longest-lived were blues musicians. Perhaps singing about all that sorrow was cathartic. Isak Dinesen said that all sorrows can be borne if you put them into a story.

"Dave's relationship with music may have been the one relationship he had that was trouble-free," a former bandmate told me. "Music was the one thing that he was so much better at than almost everyone else. He could have been even more famous and more skilled, but that would have involved actually working at it, and Dave always preferred to take the easy way. I think that alcohol and drugs replaced music as the one true relationship that Dave had in his life. When he considered what he was facing—a new, regular job, not playing professionally anymore, having to stay sober to please Katherine, and getting older, it was a burden that getting high could not ease. I believe that what he wanted was to be that twenty-five-year-old hotshot musician who could party all night, charm the women and make the men laugh. Music allowed him to do that and for so much of his life, he and music were inseparable."

There was a long period where music and drugs co-existed happily. All across the continent, kids were getting stoned and listening to music, and finding a depth in the lyrics of Jethro Tull they hadn't divined when straight. David would sit stoned with the headphones on and wait for the moment in David Bowie's "Suffragette City" when that chord went from one headphone to the other, actually travelling through his marijuana-tinged brain. Drugs were a key part of listening to the Grateful Dead, Yes and Pink Floyd, a virtual requirement for Emerson Lake and Palmer.

In the end, drugs proved a more stubborn bond than music, which I think had become like a stale marriage. When David came back to Calgary, he used to jam with old friends, and one of them remarked that he seemed more interested in getting high than in playing music.

John Russon, a philosophy professor at the University of Guelph, used a musical analogy to analyze boredom. In order to experience music, to hear a melody, we have to be able to retain the notes that came before whatever note we are hearing. "All our experiences," he wrote, "carry on something like this melodic, harmonic and rhythmic flow, whereby one moment seems to grow out of the last and melt into the next in a way that keeps the tune going." But people who are suicidal don't necessarily hear a melody, just the one isolated note. Without the context of the notes that came before and the anticipation of the notes to come, that note is tuneless, devoid of joy or meaning.

The sheer weight of days is felt by many of us. Kierkegaard described boredom as a despairing refusal to be oneself, and said it was the root of all evil. He died in 1855, more than a century before the Age of Boredom really began to flower, before gaming, before five hundred channels and the Internet, before the possibilities for stimulation were limitless. These tools only highlight the power and complexity of boredom. Endless images, noise, sex and drugs can provide temporary relief from boredom, but few things can kill it. Studies show that loneliness declines with increased face-to-face contact, but it increases with a greater number of online interactions. Social media may be social in name only.

A study showed that suicidal people experience time differently. They fear the future, don't want to examine what may be an unhappy past, and as a result are mired in an endless, grim present. They see time the way the very bored see it: something that moves too slowly, a relentless presence that is oppressive, even sinister.

Clinically, boredom has been defined as "experience without qualities." For most of us, this can be something like waiting for a bus without having anything to read, but for people who are suicidal, it applies to life. The philosopher Seneca, who eventually killed himself, said, "How long the same things? Surely I will yawn, I will sleep, I will eat, I will be thirsty, I will be cold, I will be hot. . . . But do all things go in a circle? Night overcomes day, day night, summer gives way to autumn, winter presses on autumn, which is checked by spring. All things pass that they may return. I do nothing new, I see nothing new. . . . There are many who judge living not painful but empty."

I suspect that was the case with David. He stumbled into an emptiness he was unable to fill. You get bored with smoking and drinking, and you get bored when you quit those things. You get bored sleeping around and bored in your marriage. Boredom can be defined as vividly imagining a mundane future so that each day becomes a bland reading of that script. Life suddenly stretched before David like a Beckett play.

Both music and drugs were an escape from boredom, but escape was an ongoing theme in his life. The escape my cousin and I had engineered for him when he was ten, using knotted sheets and lowering him out the window, was only the first of many. He escaped his marriage, escaped the city, his family. When he was onstage, he experienced a suspension of reality or at least created a temporary bulwark against it. Drugs and alcohol offered an escape. He even escaped from Anna Mae, someone he didn't want to escape from. It was a habit.

Arthur Schopenhauer thought that boredom was the enemy of happiness. "If life—the craving for which is the very essence of our being—were possessed of any positive intrinsic value," he wrote, "there would be no such thing as boredom at all: mere existence would satisfy us in itself, and we should want for nothing."

But we do want. Longing is the human condition. Most of us want something—to be taller, smarter, younger, richer. To be loved, to have mastered an instrument, to have learned another language. We want to have an affair *and* to preserve our marriage. We want things that are contradictory, dramatic and reassuring. Some of us cannot reconcile the contradictions.

THE RIVER REDUX

I was back in Winnipeg for Christmas, my whole family spending it at my sister's house in our old neighbourhood. On a cold afternoon, I went for a walk along the Red River with my two children, dragging our toboggan. The river was frozen, a foot of snow on the ground. The dense woods that had been filled with mystery when I played in them as a child had been radically thinned to an orderly glade. The city used to spray insecticide to deal with the swarming mosquito population that rose up every spring. An ancient flatbed truck with a machine we called the fogger chugged through the neighbourhood, leaving a billowing trail of poisonous DDT. We ran behind, wearing World War II–vintage gas masks that didn't have oxygen canisters, breathing in the carcinogens. So little seemed dangerous back then.

Now so much feels dangerous. My children are thirteen and nineteen, their early fragility long gone, replaced by a new version. The world is faster and more complex and riven with fears that didn't exist in my childhood, though the Manichean struggle of my childhood—democracy versus Russia—has been revived. There was a special bell for our nuclear drills at Oakenwald Elementary School, signalling us out into the hall, where we sat against the walls, cross-legged, our heads in our laps. We were told to keep our heads down for five minutes, the first few of those minutes surprisingly suspense-filled, the last merely uncomfortable. I remember looking up to see our teacher, a stolid, middle-aged woman in a print dress, looking distracted and blasé about our impending nuclear deaths. She had told us that Winnipeg was the centre of the continent and Khrushchev would likely strike us first. The schoolyard physics expert said if you held your breath just as the bomb hit, you'd get through the worst of it.

Once more there is a belligerent Russian leader, though now he is flanked globally by a dozen fanatics. There are more than sixteen-thousand nuclear weapons among nine countries. America is run by a failed developer whose messy adolescent ego hovers over the button, and the Doomsday Clock is set at two minutes to midnight. The economy is devolving, the climate shifting. It is the Age of Underemployment, the Age of Indifference, the Age of Pornography. So I worry.

That Christmas we tobogganed on the dike that had been built to protect our neighbourhood after the 1950 flood, a modest run. When I was a child, every year grown-ups built a run that went all the way from the community clubhouse down to the Red River. There was a big turn that was banked. One year they iced the run, some father simply turning on the hose. On a dare, I went down it on my skates, hitting the bank and flying into the air and landing in the snow like a dart. Others followed until someone got hurt, the standard operating procedure for any new game, born of our innate need to manufacture danger in that placid time.

It was cold and my kids went down the hill dutifully, though happily. They have sunny dispositions, for which I am deeply grateful. A capacity for joy, an increasingly precious commodity. Those happy faces. Perhaps the sociologists are right and their expectations are lower. Neither of them expects a job for life. Few people want one. They don't have the same attachment to things. Half their friends' parents are divorced. They aren't buoyed by the same structures; religion is an abstraction, television is already gone from their lives—they watch shows streamed on their computers. Everything has a short shelf life—technology, cultural trends, musical acts, marriage. I wonder what they will be nostalgic for.

The sun was already low, a pale blur to the west, the dull light of a winter afternoon. On the way back, we passed the rink I used to play on. I thought it would be crowded, as it was in memory, a chaotic shinny game in progress, the players calling out their own heroics as I had done (*Gillmor lets go a cannonading shot . . .*). But there were only two kids playing; the rest of the neighbourhood kids were inside their homes, warm, likely in front of a screen.

A friend once told me that the tragedy of living in the city you grew up in was that you were robbed of nostalgia. Coming back to the city of my childhood, dozens of names and faces and images leap out. Peripheral characters—the girl who wet her pants in fifth grade, the teacher who threw chalk brushes, the boy who threw up during "God Save the Queen," our mournful janitor coming by and throwing sawdust over the mess. The pretty girl, the tough guy, the blighted kids who lingered on the fringes of everything, unathletic, academically uninclined, socially shunned. Their names an endless string. What had become of all of them? I had scant news, an occasional name from the past emerging on Facebook.

The forest was empty and still. You couldn't build a fort here now because everything would be in plain sight. Our first forts were essentially clearings in the underbrush, slightly reinforced with branches, secretive and barely defined. It was an extreme application of the Wrightian idea of breaking down the barrier between inside and outside, which he had done at Fallingwater with the extensive use of glass and the rock he had incorporated into the interior. Our forts became more ambitious, though. One was built around a fallen tree. We chopped off the underlying branches and wove them into the remaining branches to form a canopy, then covered it in leaves as camouflage.

My downfall was celebrating our ingenuity by showing too many people where this fort was. Someone told someone who told the neighbourhood bully, who wrecked it. We rebuilt far into the forest. Wrecking and building forts went on all summer. Sometimes my brother and I were allied in this and sometimes we were adversaries. I can recall the sense of betrayal I felt after discreetly slipping through the woods to find my fort destroyed.

I believed time spent in every new fort would be superior to time spent in the previous fort. The moment when Susan Thompson took off all her clothes, for example, would be less confusing (but just as weirdly exhilarating) in the new fort than it had been in the old fort. The bully wouldn't find it this time. It would be a refuge. The idea of refuge is elemental to a child; witness the number of children's books with the word "secret" in the title. The forts were my first attempts at constructing a world, one that had advantages over the larger world (chiefly freedom and a society limited to people I liked).

In one of my last forts, I used salvaged plywood for a roof, then covered it meticulously with leaves. One of the walls was a discarded door. This hardening was to insulate us from atomic attack. The Russians never did attack, but on a hot August afternoon, a prairie thunderstorm approached and my brother and I sought refuge in the fort, huddled with the neighbour's dog, waiting for the worst to pass.

I could see David in this landscape as I walked home with my children. The uncomplicated version from that uncomplicated time. I remembered a Halloween, the snow falling gently, David dressed as a hobo, whiskers dabbed on with a mascara pen, a crushed hat. I was a lion tamer. We carried pillowcases to collect candy in. We would get a deeply resented apple from some houses. Chocolate bars were rare. David ate as we walked, not wanting it to end, going from house to house forever.

I could see him lying on the carpet watching our black and white TV, his head resting in his hands as Bullwinkle flickered greyly on the screen. Walking through the tall grass in the meadow by the river in summer, the locusts springing before him. Running alongside me behind the fogger, happily breathing the poison. Then scattering his ashes in the west, ten of us, each with our handful of David.

It was late, and my children and I cut through Wildwood to get home. It was cold, getting dark, and I was grateful to see the light coming through the window.

ACKNOWLEDGEMENTS

Suicide is a boundless, complex subject. It deeply affects Indigenous communities, the military, adolescents and the elderly, but here I have chosen to keep my focus narrow, to an area I have some experience with: the white boomer male.

I am grateful to the Canada Council and the Ontario Arts Council for their generous support, which made this book possible. I am indebted to all those who graciously gave their time and expertise—the sociologists, psychiatrists, suicidologists, friends and David's friends who agreed to talk to me. I am grateful to my sister and parents for their unwavering support during what was a difficult project. My thanks to Jackie Kaiser at Westwood Creative Artists for her astute reading of early drafts. As always, thank you to Anne Collins for her heroic editorial efforts, patience and wisdom. And, finally, thank you to my wife, Grazyna, for her ongoing support.

DON GILLMOR is one of Canada's most accomplished writers. He is the author of the bestselling, award-winning two-volume *Canada: A People's History,* and his journalism on suicide has earned him both a National Newspaper Award and a National Magazine Award. Gillmor's other books include the novels *Kanata, Mount Pleasant* and *Long Change,* which were published to critical acclaim, and nine books for children, two of which were nominated for the Governor General's Literary Award. He lives in Toronto with his wife and two children.